HIJACKED

HIJACKED

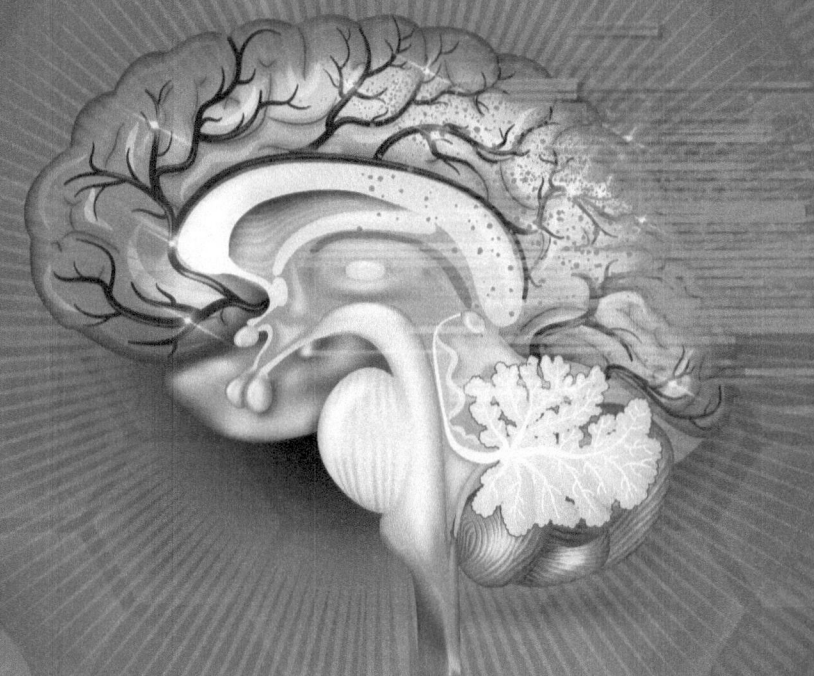

How Digital Distraction Took Over
Your Mind — and the PRECEPT
Framework to Take It Back

JIM KOETTING

HIJACKED
How Digital Distraction Took Over Your Mind—And the PRECEPT Framework to Take it Back

Copyright © 2025 by Jim Koetting

Book Cover Design by Brittany Becker and Bojan Rekovic
Interior Layout and Design by Brittany Becker

ISBN: 979-8-9942374-0-3 *Softcover*
ISBN: 979-8-9942374-2-7 *Hardcover*
ISBN: 979-8-9942374-1-0 *Ebook*

Published by:
CEOM Publishing
1228 W. 62nd Street, Kansas City, MO 64113
https://ceompublishing.com

CEOM | PUBLISHING

To Barb, my wife of 32 years—
my greatest blessing, my steady guide,
and the one who never stopped believing in me.

And to our daughters, Morgan and Madi --
your voices as writers inspired me
to find the courage to use mine.

Contents

A Note to the Reader

This book is about small steps, not grand gestures. It is about lighting a path out of the forest one tiny flame at a time. Change rarely begins with dramatic breakthroughs. It begins with one discipline that leads to another, and then another, until new habits take root and a new way of living becomes possible.

Everything in these pages comes from lived experience. These ideas are not theories I developed in isolation—they are the practices that pulled me out of my own forest and continue to work in my life today. They are also the same practices I see working with the coaching clients I mentor, the leaders I consult, and the audiences I speak to. The patterns repeat, and so do the results: small, steady disciplines have the power to rewire the brain and reshape a life.

I am not a neuroscientist or a clinician. I am simply someone who followed a broken compass for too long and had to learn how to build a new one. I am not offering diagnoses or guarantees. I am sharing what has been proven—not in laboratories, but in kitchens, offices, meetings, families, late-night conversations, and quiet moments when someone finally decides they want their life back.

The science in this book is intentionally simple. If you want a deeper dive into the research on habits, dopamine, and neural pathways, I've included resources for further study. But the heart of this book is practical: small steps, taken consistently, create new pathways in the brain. And new pathways lead to new outcomes.

You do not need to see the entire path right now. You only need to see the next step.

If you're ready, let's take it together.

Preface

The Faulty Compass in the Forest

There comes a moment in life when you realize you're deep in a forest you never meant to enter. The trees are thick, the light is dim, and every direction looks the same. In your hand is a compass, but something is wrong. The needle jumps and spins, pulled by invisible magnets you can't see—fear, old habits, loneliness, and the promise of "just one more" tugging it in different directions. No matter how hard you stare at it, the compass won't settle.

It's a strange thing to discover that the tool you trusted to guide you—the way you think, decide, and cope—has been quietly leading you off course. Sometimes the only way out of the forest is to admit that your compass isn't pointing north anymore, and that you need a new way to navigate. A new direction. A new mind. A new path.

The forest doesn't change just because you wish it would. The compass won't fix itself. The way out begins the moment you choose one honest step in a new direction.

In the fall of 1989, I reached a point in my life where everything was falling apart. I didn't want to quit drinking; I wanted to drink like a normal person. That is the quiet fantasy of every alcoholic. We don't dream of sobriety. We dream of control. We dream of being able to cut back, slow down, drink casually, sip responsibly, and still enjoy all the things we imagine others enjoy. But deep down, most of us know the truth long before we admit it: that dream never comes true.

I didn't meet Tom, the man who would become my AA sponsor, because of courage or clarity. I met him because I was in pain. Real pain. The kind you can't hide from yourself in the quiet moments. My mom had been nagging me about my drinking for a long time—subtle comments, passive-aggressive hints, little stings meant to push me toward change. My dad, who I was living with at the time, was more direct. He didn't sugarcoat things. He didn't dance around the point. He told me straight that my life was going downhill fast.

And he was right.

I had no money. I didn't like my job. My relationships were shallow, built on jokes and drinks rather than trust and honesty. I had drinking buddies, not friends. I was anxious, depressed, constantly stressed about bills, and increasingly aware of a deep emptiness in my soul that I couldn't soothe. Loneliness sat with me like a shadow that wouldn't leave. My life sucked, and I knew it.

The only reason I reached out to Tom was because I didn't know where else to turn. My mom gave me his number. I remember calling him and hoping—secretly—that he would agree to meet me that night so I could get this over with quickly. But he didn't. He told me he could meet in a couple of days. Those days felt like an eternity. Two long days to sit with the truth I was trying to outrun.

When the night finally came, we met at a small table—just two men, smoking cigarettes and drinking bad coffee, talking for three straight hours. He started by telling me his story. Not preaching. Not diagnosing. Just telling the truth of his own life. And then we talked. I told him everything, or at least everything I was ready to admit. He didn't flinch. He didn't judge. He didn't try to fix me.

By the end of that conversation, I walked away believing I could control my drinking. If I could control it, then I wasn't an alcoholic. That was the logic my addicted brain clung to.

But a few days later, I was binge drinking again. And I was back on cocaine. That was the night I proved to myself what nobody else could prove for me: I could not control my drinking. I had crossed the line, and the line wasn't moving back for me.

Fast-forward thirty-six years.

Today, I understand things I didn't have the language for back then. I understand neuroplasticity—the brain's ability to rewire itself. I understand habit loops. I understand dopamine and reward pathways. But back in 1989, I didn't know any of that. I was just trying to survive. And what ultimately saved my life wasn't willpower. It was replacement.

I replaced the bar with an AA meeting. I replaced isolation with conversation. I replaced drifting with prayer. I replaced numbing out with reading. I replaced anxiety with exercise. I replaced chaos with journaling and capturing my thoughts. I replaced addictive habits with meaningful habits. I replaced noise with thinking.

Every replacement was a small step toward building a different brain. A different life. A different future.

And here's where this book begins to take shape.

In recent years, I realized I had fallen into a different kind of addiction—screens. At one point, I completely stopped all social media and screen scrolling. Cold turkey. But eventually, I got sucked right back in. The same patterns, the same dopamine hits, the same empty rewards. It wasn't alcohol this time. It wasn't cocaine. But the mechanism was the same. The brain doesn't care whether the dopamine comes from a bottle or a screen. If it fires the reward circuit, it hooks you.

That's when I realized something. I needed to approach screens the same way I approached sobriety. Not by trying harder. Not by white-knuckling my way through willpower. Not by "just putting the phone down."

I needed to replace screen time with something else. Something better. Something that would build me rather than drain me.

That is where the PRECEPT framework was born. A simple structure for replacing screen time with the practices that build joy, clarity, connection, and strength. Prayer. Reading. Exercise. Capturing. Engaging. Practicing. Thinking.

Because the truth is this: screen time gives us short dopamine hits, but it rewires our brains in ways that slowly rob us of deeper joys. We are digitally connected but disconnected from each other. Kids are growing up without the ability to have real conversations. We don't call; we text. We don't share our real lives; we post curated versions of them. We compare ourselves to illusions and then feel like we're not measuring up. We join social media or political tribes that reward outrage and mockery. We see the best memes and lose the ability to step back and see the forest for the trees.

Our screens have hijacked our attention, our emotions, our relationships, and our time.

This book is about taking them back.

My goal is not to guilt you, shame you, or scare you. My goal is to give you practical tools that anyone can use to reclaim their time, rewire their brain, and rediscover connection with themselves and others. Tools that can help you or someone you love step out of mindless scrolling and into a more meaningful life.

Before we begin, I want to offer a simple disclaimer. This is my story. This is what worked for me. I am not making medical claims or guaranteeing anyone's results.

I am sharing what hijacked my life, what saved it, and what I have watched change the lives of others.

If you are ready, let's take the next step together.

Introduction

The Sixteen-Year Sentence

THE MOST DANGEROUS PRISONS ARE THE ONES WE DON'T REALIZE WE'RE LIVING IN.

Mike never expected to find himself standing in a courtroom, waiting for a judge to speak words that felt heavier than anything he had carried before. He wasn't a violent man or a criminal. He was middle-aged, tired, overwhelmed—one of countless people who drifted through their days feeling more numb than alive. But as the judge entered and took his seat, the quiet in the room settled on Mike's shoulders like a lead blanket.

"Sixteen years," the judge said, adjusting his glasses as if the number were merely procedural.

The words hit Mike with a physical jolt. For a moment he wondered if he had misheard. Sixteen years meant missing graduations and birthdays. It meant children growing up without him, routines shifting in ways he'd never witness, a life unfolding behind glass. Sixteen years meant absence. It meant silence. It meant losing time he could never earn back.

He stood there, stunned, until his attorney guided him out of the courtroom and into a small adjoining room. The fluorescent light hummed overhead. Four cardboard boxes sat on the table between them. The attorney's face softened.

"There's another way to serve your time," he said quietly. "You won't be behind bars. You'll be serving your sentence at home."

Mike looked at the boxes, confused, waiting for the catch.

The attorney pulled the first box closer. Inside was a television. He opened the second: a laptop. The third: an iPad. The fourth: a smartphone. Mike's confusion deepened.

"You'll spend a few hours a day with these," the attorney said. "Two and a half hours scrolling, two and a half watching news, shows, streaming—whatever you prefer. Keep that up every day, and over the course of your life, you'll serve the full sixteen-year sentence."

He paused, letting the implication settle.

"Most people already do," he added. "They never notice the bars going up. They never feel the door closing. But it happens—slowly, quietly—one minute at a time."

Mike slid a hand across the smooth edge of the television, the plastic cold against his skin. Sixteen years. Not in a single stretch, but scattered across a lifetime in increments too small to protest. Minutes lost to scrolling in bed. Hours swallowed by news cycles. Evenings dissolved into shows he barely remembered. Years spent staring at glowing rectangles while life unfolded somewhere else.

His attorney watched him closely. "These devices won't chain your hands," he said. "They'll chain your attention. And once your attention is gone, everything else follows—relationships, purpose, presence, joy. The sentence isn't obvious, but it's real."

The comment lingered in the quiet room. Mike realized, with a discomfort that bordered on grief, that he had already begun serving the sentence long before he ever heard it spoken. He had traded conversations for background noise, relationships for notifications, purpose for distraction. The worst part was that he hadn't made those choices consciously. He had drifted into them.

He closed the lids of the cardboard boxes one by one. The room seemed smaller now, tighter. A thin thread of panic wound its way through his chest, not because of the judge's words, but because of the realization that he had willingly surrendered pieces of his life without understanding the cost.

But beneath the panic was something else. A whisper of clarity. The knowledge that if an invisible sentence existed, there had to be a way out of it.

Escape wouldn't come from throwing away the screens or declaring digital bankruptcy. It would begin the way any real change begins—with a single honest step. One decision to reclaim a small corner of his attention. One act of replacing a draining habit with one that restored him. One moment of waking up.

This book begins at that moment.

It is an invitation to step out of the unseen prison so many of us inhabit. To rebuild the mind through small disciplines. To rediscover presence, purpose, connection, and clarity—one deliberate step at a time.

This is not a book about trying harder. It's a book about choosing differently. About recognizing the sentence we've been quietly serving and learning how to walk out of it.

One small decision. One habit. One new path. Repeated long enough to change a life.

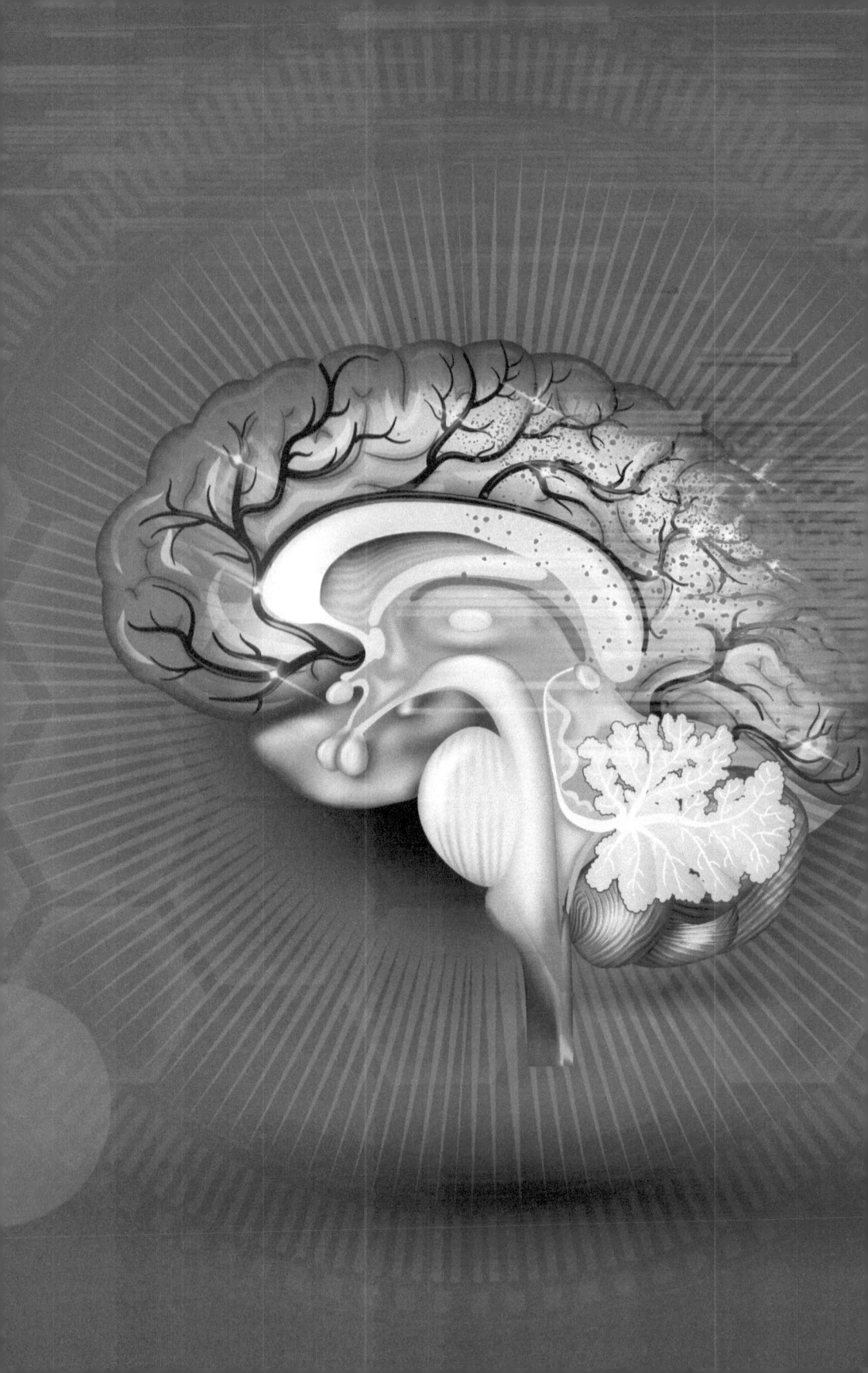

PART I

The Invisible War for Your Attention

CHAPTER 1

The Distraction Economy

Why We Lose Ourselves

I t was 2:17 a.m. when Michael's eyes opened, and the first thing he noticed was that his body felt braced, as if it had been holding tension all night. Nothing had startled him awake. The house was quiet, the heat clicked on and off the way it always did, and still his mind ran like a motor that wouldn't idle down. He lay there trying to locate the problem—because surely there had to be one. People don't wake up tense for no reason.

That's what made it so frustrating. Nothing "big" had happened. Work had its usual demands, but nothing catastrophic; bills were paid; his family was fine. No crisis, no blow-up, no dramatic moment he could point to and say, *That's when I started coming apart.* Yet here he was in the dark, eyes open, thoughts skipping from one unfinished thread to another.

Without thinking, he reached for his phone. It wasn't a choice so much as a practiced movement, like scratching an itch before you realize you've been bitten. The screen lit his face. He told himself he was checking quickly, just enough to quiet his mind and get back to sleep. But the quiet didn't come. One notification led to another. A headline tugged at his curiosity. An email reminded him of a meeting. A meeting reminded him of something he hadn't sent. He opened an app to note it, saw a message, answered it, and before long, he was scrolling—absorbing information he wouldn't remember tomorrow, feeding a restlessness that was already wearing him down.

When he finally put the phone down, he felt no better. He felt more awake, not less—more tense, not calmer. Twenty minutes had vanished without drama, and something about that invisibility bothered him. The time wasn't stolen violently; it simply disappeared, the way sand disappears when you don't realize your hand is open.

He rolled onto his side and stared into the dark again. The same question returned, quieter now but heavier, as if it had been waiting underneath everything else: *When did it get like this?* And then, almost immediately, a second question: *Why can't I seem to stop?*

Most people do not lose themselves all at once. There is rarely a single collapse, a single day when the floor gives way. Losing yourself is slower than that—quieter, gradual, almost invisible. It happens the way a shoreline erodes: one small wave at a time, a little here and a little there, nothing noticeable in the moment and everything noticeable in hindsight.

At first, you don't even realize anything is slipping. You still show up. You still perform. You still take care of what needs to be taken care of. Life remains functional. But underneath, something begins to shift. You find yourself tired for reasons you can't explain. Your patience shortens. Your creativity dulls. Your attention breaks easily, not because you've become lazy, but because your mind has learned to live in fragments. You might even wake in the middle of the night with a spinning mind and a tight chest, confused by the tension because nothing "big" has happened.

Then the drift begins to show in places that matter. You react more quickly than you mean to. Decisions feel heavier. Tasks pile up faster than you can clear them. Relationships become more complicated, not necessarily because people have changed, but because you have less emotional margin. Slowly, you drift into a version of yourself that feels slightly off—less grounded, less clear, less present. Not broken, exactly. Just... displaced.

This chapter is about that drift. Not a catastrophe. The drift. Because you can't reclaim your life if you don't understand what's been taking it.

The Silent Thief of Modern Life

We often assume people lose themselves because of major stress: a crisis, a loss, a conflict, a failure. Those moments matter, and sometimes they accelerate the drift. But most people don't begin losing themselves in dramatic moments. They start losing themselves through something much smaller, much more common, and much easier to dismiss: distraction.

Not the loud kind that screams for attention, but the quiet kind that slides into the cracks of ordinary life. The notifications you didn't ask for. The scrolling was supposed to last thirty seconds. The "quick check" turns into ten minutes and then into a pattern. The constant switching—task to message, message to headline, headline to video—because the mind has been trained to chase novelty like a thirsty person chasing drops of water.

We tell ourselves it's normal. We tell ourselves it's necessary. We tell ourselves we're staying informed, connected, productive. But distraction doesn't merely take time; it takes the inner conditions that make a meaningful life possible. It steals deep focus and turns creative work into cognitive sputtering. It interrupts rest, leaving the body tired while the mind stays wired. It crowds out reflection, leaving wisdom no place to form. It fractures presence, so you can sit in the same room with the people you love and still feel strangely elsewhere.

A LINE WORTH REMEMBERING

Distraction doesn't just steal your time. It steals your ability to live on purpose.

And it does this in minutes. Minutes that stack. Minutes that quietly replace the practices that once made you feel alive.

What begins as a harmless habit can become the structure of an entire day. Five minutes becomes fifteen, and fifteen becomes thirty. Thirty becomes two hours—and two hours becomes the space where your real life used to live: reading, thinking, praying, creating, connecting, resting. Distraction isn't simply a bad habit. For many people, it becomes a replacement for a life.

The Distraction Economy: Engineered Fracture

It would be comforting if drift were merely a discipline problem, because then the solution would be simple: "Try harder. Be more focused. Make better choices." Discipline matters, but that explanation is too small for what's happening to us. You are living inside an environment designed to make focus harder and craving easier, and it works so well because it rarely feels like an attack.

The modern economy has learned how to monetize attention. Not merely to win your attention once, but to keep winning it—over and over, in smaller and smaller increments. The success of many platforms depends on one thing: how often you return and how long you stay. Notifications pull you back. Infinite scroll keeps the feed going. Recommendation engines learn what captures you and then serve it back to you, refined. The result is a world in which your mind is constantly being invited—sometimes gently, sometimes aggressively—to leave the present moment.

This doesn't mean technology is evil. It means it is not neutral. It has incentives. And those incentives don't automatically align with your well-being.

What makes this so difficult to recognize is that none of it has to feel dramatic. In fact, the system functions best when it feels normal. A small check here. A brief scroll there. A quick answer. A few minutes of relief. You don't notice the erosion because each wave is small.

But attention is the gateway to everything you say you want: clarity, creativity, connection, faith, wisdom, peace. When attention becomes fractured, those outcomes become harder to reach—not because you don't care, but because you can't stay in one place long enough for depth to form.

That is the invisible war for your attention. It's not fought with weapons you can see. It's fought with design you barely notice.

The Three Ways People Drift Away From Themselves

Drift has patterns. It shows up in different lives—different responsibilities, different backgrounds, different personalities—but the same currents keep pulling people in the same direction. Most people can't name the current while it's happening. They only see the result: the fog, the impatience, the strange weariness, the sense that something good has thinned out inside them.

In my experience, the drift usually enters through one of three doors. Many people recognize themselves in at least one. Quite a few discover they've been living in all three.

The first door is busyness.

Busyness can look like virtue. It often carries the costume of responsibility: work ethic, availability, sacrifice, productivity. From the outside, a busy person appears reliable. From the inside, busyness can feel like staying afloat. If you keep moving, you don't sink. If you keep producing, you don't have to sit with what you feel. If you keep the schedule full, you don't have to hear what your own mind might say when the noise finally shuts off.

Sometimes busyness is a calendar that never breathes, loaded with meetings, obligations, errands, and commitments that seemed reasonable one at a time. But busyness doesn't always live on paper. Sometimes it lives in the mind—an invisible treadmill of thoughts, reminders, and half-finished worries that keeps a person "on" even when they're sitting still. That internal busyness can be the most exhausting kind, because the body rests while the mind keeps running.

Maria fits here.

She isn't lazy and she isn't failing. She's the kind of person who handles things. She remembers birthdays, schedules appointments, manages details other people don't even notice. She loves her family deeply, and that love expresses itself in doing what needs to be done. But somewhere along the way, her life became a room where every surface is covered. There's no place to set anything down—not physically, and not emotionally either. When she finally gets a quiet moment, her mind doesn't soften; it accelerates, because quiet is where all the unfinished things come looking for her. It feels easier to stay busy than to sit still, because stillness threatens to bring up questions she doesn't have time to answer.

The second door is escape.

Everyone needs relief. The human nervous system wasn't built to carry tension without interruption. The issue isn't that people want to unwind; it's what they choose to unwind into. Healthy escape restores you. It returns you to your life with more strength than you had before. Unhealthy escape numbs you. It offers quick relief and long-term damage.

Screens are unusually good at numbing because they require almost nothing from you. They ask for no courage, no vulnerability, no effort, no patience. They offer stimulation on demand, and the brain interprets stimulation as reward. It's why a tired mind reaches for a phone the way a thirsty person reaches for water. In the moment, it feels like relief. Over time, it becomes a dependency—not always in the clinical sense, but in the very practical sense that you don't know how to come down without it.

Michael fits here.

Michael doesn't think of himself as someone who "escapes." He would tell you he's just decompressing. And he is—at least at first. A hard day ends, and the phone appears. A stressful moment comes and a quick scroll smooths the edge off his feelings. A pause shows up and he fills it. In isolation, each moment looks harmless.

But the moments don't stay isolated. They stack. They form a rhythm. The phone becomes his default way to regulate stress, which means the part of him that used to regulate stress—reflection, movement, prayer, conversation, silence—gets less practice. The screen doesn't merely distract him; it becomes his primary method of coping. And when the screen becomes the coping strategy, life begins to feel like something you endure and then escape from, rather than something you inhabit.

The third door is forgetting.

Not dramatic forgetting, the kind that shocks you. Gradual forgetting, the kind that happens so slowly you don't notice what's gone until you try to reach for it.

People forget what makes them feel alive. They forget what restores them. They forget what they were building before they became busy and reactive. They forget the practices that once gave their life weight and texture: reading something that requires attention, praying without rushing, walking without headphones, creating without needing to post it, talking with someone and actually being there.

These practices may seem small, but they are not trivial. They are the backbone of identity. They are how a person stays grounded in who they are. And when they are crowded out—first occasionally, then regularly, then almost completely—your sense of self doesn't explode. It dissolves. Like ink in water: still there, but harder to see.

This is why drift can be so confusing. From the outside, life appears intact. From the inside, it feels diluted.

Two Lives, One Current (Maria and Michael)

Maria's drift doesn't announce itself with a disaster. It shows up in the small distortions of daily life. She finds herself snapping at her kids over things that wouldn't have bothered her before, then feeling ashamed about it later. She feels tired even after sleep, as if the body rested but the mind never stopped working. She stays "on" all day and then lies down at night with a head full of invisible tabs still open. Even when the house is quiet, her nervous system isn't. She isn't choosing to be impatient or scattered; she is living in a state where patience and steadiness require more effort than they used to.

Michael's drift shows up differently, but it grows from the same root. He goes through his day and checks his phone so often he stops noticing he's doing it. He answers messages while half-listening to conversations. He opens an app for a purpose and forgets why he opened it. He finds it harder to read, harder to pray, harder to start something creative without quickly getting restless. When he tries to focus, it's like trying to hold water in his hands: he can do it for a moment, but it keeps slipping away. He tells himself he needs more discipline, but discipline isn't the full story. He's been training his mind, day after day, to live in fragments.

THE DRIFT TEST

Ask yourself one honest question: When was the last time you felt fully present—and didn't have to fight for it? Not productive. Not busy. Not entertained. Present. Clear. Steady.

In both cases, everything on the surface keeps functioning, but nothing feels like it's thriving.

That's drift. And it's so common now that we treat it like weather—something you tolerate, something you complain about, something you assume you can't change. But drift is not weather. Drift is a current. Currents can be understood, resisted, and navigated.

The Hidden Cost of Distraction

Most people measure distraction the wrong way. They treat it like a time problem, as if the primary loss is simply the hours that evaporate—thirty minutes here, an hour there, a weekend that disappears faster than it should. Time matters, of course, but time is only the most visible cost. It's the cost you can count.

The deeper cost is what you can't easily quantify.

Distraction reduces your inner life the way constant wind reduces a fire. Not by extinguishing it all at once, but by keeping it from ever fully catching. It weakens clarity, because clarity requires sustained attention long enough for patterns to emerge. It weakens creativity, because creativity isn't born in constant stimulation; it's born in the quiet space where thoughts can collide, combine, and surprise you. It weakens presence, because presence is not merely being in a room—it's being available in that room, internally and emotionally.

Distraction affects emotional regulation as well. A mind trained to switch constantly becomes less able to stay with a feeling long enough to understand it. It learns to dodge discomfort, to seek interruption as medicine. The problem is that interruption doesn't heal discomfort. It only postpones it. And postponed feelings don't disappear; they store themselves in the body as tension, irritability, numbness, and fatigue.

THE PRINCIPLE

Distraction doesn't destroy your life in one dramatic moment. It slowly replaces the parts of your life where meaning used to form.

A distracted life does something else that many people don't notice until it's advanced. It takes the edges off life. It turns moments that should be rich into moments that feel thin. A meal becomes something you eat while half-reading. A conversation becomes something you do while checking. A quiet evening becomes something you fill. The days keep functioning, but they lose their flavor.

The greatest damage of distraction is not that it costs you minutes.

It's that it costs you depth.

And depth is where transformation happens.

Why Transformation Requires Depth

Transformation is one of the most misunderstood words in modern life. We tend to picture it as something fast: a breakthrough, a decision, a surge of motivation, a new habit that sticks because you finally "got serious." But most real change doesn't happen through surges. It happens through depth—through repeated practices, through honest reflection, through time spent with yourself, through the slow strengthening of attention and intention.

Depth doesn't require perfection, but it does require space.

It requires silence long enough for you to hear what's true beneath the noise. It requires reflection long enough for you to untangle what you feel. It requires repetition long enough for the nervous system to learn a new rhythm. It requires emotional engagement, because change doesn't stick when it's only intellectual. It requires purpose, because without purpose you're simply managing behavior rather than building a life.

These are the very conditions the distraction economy interrupts.

Screens don't merely take your time. They take the gaps. They take the small stretches where your mind would have settled. They take the moments where you might have prayed, thought, written, walked, breathed, listened, noticed. The device in your pocket is not only a tool; it's a gatekeeper. It decides, again and again, whether a moment becomes deep or becomes shallow.

ANOTHER LINE WORTH REMEMBERING

You don't become what you intend. You become what you repeatedly practice.

When a person lives for long enough without depth, the soul begins to starve. Not in any mystical sense you have to agree with, but in the practical sense: the inner self needs nourishment to remain strong. When it is fed only stimulation, it becomes restless. When it is fed only urgency, it becomes anxious. When it is never allowed to settle, it begins to forget what it feels like to be whole.

This is why so many people can't simply "be more disciplined." Discipline matters, but discipline isn't the starting line when your environment is engineered to pull you toward fragmentation. The starting line is awareness—seeing the system for what it is—and then rebuilding your life from the inside out through practices that restore depth.

Transformation does not come from speed. It comes from depth. And depth is not a personality trait. It is a practice.

The Good News You May Not Believe Yet

If you feel scattered, foggy, depleted, or distant from yourself, the natural assumption is that something is wrong with you. You may think you've become weaker, less motivated, less capable, less... you.

But what if you are not broken?

What if you are buried?

When a person has been distracted for years, the best parts of them don't disappear. They go under. Like a house covered by sand after a long storm, still present, still intact, but no longer visible from the surface. What you are experiencing may not be a permanent loss of identity. It may be the temporary effect of living beneath layers of noise.

Your focus is still there. Your clarity is still there. Your faith is still there. Your creativity is still there. Your peace is still there. Your leadership is still there. Your purpose is still there.

They are simply harder to access when your attention is constantly being pulled away from the very interior space where those qualities live.

This is why the solution cannot be only productivity tips. You do not need a tighter calendar or a better app to manage it. You do not need a motivational speech or a program designed to make you hustle harder. You do not need to become a different person.

You need a way back to yourself.

Not in theory. In practice.

That is what the **PRECEPT Framework** is built to give you: a grounded path back to the habits and inner strengths that make a human life sturdy again. It is not about adding more pressure. It is about reclaiming what has been slowly taken. It is about building a life that supports depth instead of constantly undermining it.

But there is one more truth you need before you move forward.

People do not change because they learn new information. People change because they remember who they were meant to be.

This book is about remembering.

Your life is not waiting for a perfect version of you. Your life is waiting for a present version of you.

POINTS TO REMEMBER

By now you may be seeing your own life in Maria, or Michael, or both. That recognition is not meant to produce shame; it is meant to produce clarity. Shame tells you that you are defective. Clarity tells you that you are human, living inside an environment designed to fragment you, and that you can choose a different path.

Most people do not lose themselves in a crisis. They lose themselves through drift—quiet, gradual, almost invisible. Distraction is not merely a habit; it is an economy. It is engineered to keep you engaged, and it succeeds by keeping your attention fractured. The cost is not only time. The cost is clarity, presence, depth, creativity, emotional steadiness, and the inner conditions required for transformation. Finally, you have not permanently lost yourself. What feels distant is more likely buried than destroyed, and buried things can be uncovered.

In the chapters ahead, we are going to stop treating your attention like an afterthought and start treating it like the foundation of your life. We will not do this through shame or frantic discipline. We will do it through a simple, grounded path—one that leads you out of drift and back into depth.

That path is the PRECEPT Framework.

And now that you can see the current, you can begin to navigate.

CHAPTER 2

The Chemistry of Disconnection

Why This Isn't Your Fault

A STORY TO START: "THE MEETING BEFORE THE MEETING"

The meeting was scheduled for nine o'clock, but Jim had been in it since six. Not in the conference room, of course. The room was still empty at six. The building was quiet. But his nervous system was already bracing the way it braced whenever something mattered. He woke early with a familiar jolt—mind awake before his body felt ready—because somewhere in him the day had already begun to demand an answer.

He made coffee and opened his phone. That wasn't a decision; it was the modern equivalent of taking a pulse. Overnight email. A text from someone who needed something "quick." A headline he didn't ask for. A short clip that made him exhale. Another clip. A message he should respond to. A notification that might be nothing but could be important. The sequence continued until he realized he was standing in the kitchen with his coffee cooling, mind already scattered, and a quiet irritation rising for no rational reason.

By the time he sat at his desk, he felt behind.

Not behind on work—behind in himself. He had the strange sense that his attention had been spent before he'd consciously chosen where to spend it. It was like arriving at the airport and discovering someone else had already used your boarding pass. He was present, technically, but his mind had been chopped into small pieces and distributed across ten different places.

He tried to focus on the meeting agenda, but his thoughts slid off the page. His body felt tense. His jaw tightened. He noticed he was holding his breath in shallow sips. He told himself, *Get it together.* He'd led teams. Built companies. Solved hard problems. He had discipline. He had grit. And yet he couldn't seem to gather himself into the steadiness he wanted to bring into the room.

On the drive in, he played the day like a film trailer in his head and felt his pulse jump at each scene. What if the numbers didn't look right? What if the conversation went sideways? What if someone challenged him in front of everyone? He wasn't afraid of the work. He was afraid of the feeling—of being exposed as less calm than he appeared.

Then, at a red light, something simple and clarifying occurred to him: he wasn't losing focus because he lacked character.

He was losing focus because he had chemistry.

Because his body was doing what bodies do when they're flooded with stimulation and stress: it was preparing for threat, seeking relief, chasing reward, and struggling to hold the kind of attention that requires internal calm.

He had been trying to solve a biological problem with willpower.

And most people are doing the same thing every day.

■　■　■　■

People blame themselves for being distracted. They call it weakness, laziness, lack of discipline. They decide the problem must be a flaw in their character, as if attention were simply a moral choice: *Just focus. Just try harder. Just stop checking. Just be more organized.*

But distraction is rarely a character issue.

Distraction is a chemistry issue.

Your brain, your body, your emotions, your cravings, your stress responses—they all run on chemistry. You are not merely fighting your phone. You are fighting your own neurobiology inside an environment designed to provoke it.

Before we go further, I want to explain why I understand this so deeply. Not from books. From experience. From survival.

My First Chemistry Lesson Came at Twenty-Two

When I was twenty-two years old, I realized I had a drinking and drug problem. That sentence sounds clean and simple now. It didn't feel simple then.

I didn't want to quit—not even a little. I loved drinking. I loved the feeling of being drunk. I loved the rush, the release, the escape. And when I added cocaine on top of that, the dopamine hit was so explosive that stopping felt impossible. You don't walk away from something that gives your brain the biggest reward it has ever tasted. You don't casually quit euphoria.

But my life was a mess. I had a problem, and it wasn't mainly a problem of morality. It was a chemistry problem. I was not bad. I was not weak. I was not broken. My brain was chasing a hit so powerful it drowned out everything else.

Getting clean was not neat. It was painful. It was messy. Some days it wasn't "one day at a time." It was fifteen minutes at a time, then one hour at a time, then one meeting at a time. By the grace of God, and the fellowship of people who had walked the same road, and the honesty of the Twelve Steps, a prison door opened for me. I walked out of it. Then I spent years helping others walk out, too.

In that season I learned something most people never fully understand: the desire to escape is not always a moral failure. Very often it is a biological reflex. Your brain seeks relief. Your brain seeks reward. Your brain seeks numbness when life becomes too much.

For me, the prison was alcohol and cocaine.

For millions of people today, the prison is smaller, quieter, and socially acceptable. It fits in your pocket. It lights up when it wants your attention.

The Modern Prison: the Screen

Social media is not "just a bad habit." It is a small, portable dopamine machine. I'm not interested in demonizing technology. I enjoy a great movie. I appreciate a funny clip. I've learned real things from smart videos and thoughtful content.

But here is the truth we have to tell: much of what you hold in your hand every day is engineered to hijack your chemistry. Not by accident. By design. And when something hijacks chemistry long enough, it becomes a prison. The bars are invisible, but the confinement is real.

I know what a chemical prison feels like. Screens can create the same patterns in a different form: compulsive checking, craving reward, emotional avoidance, anxiety spikes, depression dips, obsessively seeking relief, never feeling satisfied.

This is not weakness.

This is biology.

The Three Chemical Forces Behind Lost Focus

Let's simplify the science, because most people don't need a neuroscience degree. They need understanding. The goal here is not to overwhelm you with vocabulary; it's to remove shame by explaining what your body is doing.

There are three chemical forces at work in modern distraction: dopamine, cortisol, and the relational chemistry of connection—what many people think of as oxytocin and serotonin. You may hear these names often, but it's the pattern that matters.

A CLEARER DIAGNOSIS

You are not failing because you're undisciplined.
You're struggling because your nervous system is being trained—hour by hour—by what you repeatedly consume.

DOPAMINE: THE DRIVER OF CRAVINGS

Dopamine is often described as the "pleasure chemical," but that's not quite accurate. Dopamine is more like the chemical of anticipation. It's the engine behind *seeking*. It's what whispers, *Maybe the next thing will make you feel better. Maybe the next swipe will be the one. Maybe the next notification will finally satisfy the itch.*

Cocaine creates an extreme, unnatural spike in dopamine. That's part of what makes it so destructive. But modern technology creates something subtler and, in some ways, more pervasive: micro-spikes, repeated hundreds of times a day. Every swipe. Every "like." Every new clip. Every refresh. Every message that appears while you're trying to do something else.

Dopamine doesn't calm you. It mobilizes you.

It makes you reach, not rest. It makes you pursue, not settle. It creates motion. And motion feels like progress even when it's only stimulation.

That's why scrolling can feel like relief while quietly producing restlessness. If dopamine is the gas pedal, most people are pressing it all day without realizing it.

CORTISOL: THE STRESS AMPLIFIER

Cortisol is part of your survival system. It's the chemical that helps you respond to threat. In the right dose, it's useful. It helps you get up, take action, handle danger, push through hard moments.

But when cortisol runs high for long stretches—when your nervous system is consistently braced—your inner world begins to change. You become more irritable. More anxious. You sleep lightly or poorly. You get emotionally overwhelmed more easily. You snap faster. Your attention becomes harder to hold because the mind is scanning for trouble, not settling into depth.

Here is what most people don't notice: the more cortisol in your system, the more your body unconsciously searches for relief. And the easiest "relief" available is often the dopamine loop—one more check, one more scroll, one more hit of novelty.

This is how people get trapped in a chemistry cycle. Stress drives you toward dopamine. Dopamine fragments your attention. Fragmented attention creates more stress. And the loop tightens.

You can call it a habit. You can call it an addiction. But underneath the language is the same reality: a nervous system that has learned to self-medicate.

OXYTOCIN AND SEROTONIN: THE CHEMISTRY OF CONNECTION AND STEADINESS

There are chemicals associated with connection, safety, steadiness, gratitude, and belonging. Oxytocin is often linked to bonding and relational safety. Serotonin is often linked to mood stability and a sense of grounded wellbeing.

The important thing is not mastering the terms; it's understanding the direction of the forces. When you live in real connection—face-to-face relationships, unhurried presence, genuine conversation, meaningful touch, faithful community—your inner chemistry changes. You become steadier. You become more secure. Your cravings reduce because the nervous system experiences safety.

Screens don't build that kind of chemistry. They simulate connection while often starving it. They provide contact without communion.

Real connection does something screens can't do: it settles you.

Stillness settles you. Reflection settles you. Prayer settles you. Presence settles you. The practices that form wisdom are the practices that restore the inner chemistry of being human.

When those practices go down, cravings go up.

When steadiness goes down, seeking goes up.

And that's why so many people feel caught.

■   ■   ■   ■

Leaders Lose Influence When Chemistry Fails

A LEADERSHIP TRUTH

You can't lead people into calm you don't possess.
And you can't build cultures of focus with a nervous system trained for fragmentation.

This isn't only a personal issue. It's also a leadership issue.

When your nervous system is hijacked, leadership becomes reaction instead of wisdom. You can have the right strategy, the right words, the right plan, the right opportunities—and still show up with the wrong internal state. And people can feel that state, even if you never name it.

When you are tired, stressed, distracted, overwhelmed, anxious, and scattered, your presence weakens. There is a kind of static that enters the room with you. Teams sense it. Families sense it instantly. You lose clarity and calmness. You lose patience. You lose vision. You lose the ability to lead from wisdom rather than urgency.

Not because you are failing.

Because your chemistry is failing.

Influence is not only what you say. It's what you transmit. Your nervous system teaches other nervous systems what to expect. If you lead from steadiness, people feel steadiness. If you lead from agitation, people feel agitation. If you lead from distraction, the organization quietly becomes distracted with you.

Leadership requires presence. Presence requires regulation. Regulation requires chemistry.

That is one of the reasons the **PRECEPT Framework** exists: not to "fix" you, but to restore the internal conditions that make you focused, grounded, patient, clear, and whole.

You Cannot Willpower Your Way Out of Biology

Here is a truth most self-help books never say clearly enough: you cannot out-discipline a deregulated nervous system.

You cannot "motivate" your way past chronic anxiety. You cannot "get organized" if your brain is drowning in cortisol. You cannot "focus more" if dopamine loops have hijacked your reward system. You cannot simply "try harder" when your chemistry is sabotaging your clarity.

Trying harder is not the answer.

Trying differently is.

The PRECEPT Framework is not about raw self-control; it is about self-regulation. It is about choosing daily practices that reset your nervous system and rebuild healthy chemistry. It is about creating conditions where focus becomes possible again and presence becomes natural again.

When you understand your biology, you stop blaming yourself. And the moment shame lifts, change becomes possible.

What I Want You to Know Before We Move Forward

You are not broken. You are not weak. You are not failing. You are not defective. You are human.

Your brain is doing exactly what it was designed to do: seek relief, avoid pain, and chase reward. The problem is not you. The problem is the environment you live in—an environment that offers constant stimulation, constant urgency, and constant access to cheap rewards.

The solution is simple. Not easy—simple.

Small, grounding practices that redirect chemistry, restore clarity, and rebuild your inner life. That is what the next chapters will give you.

But first, before we begin the work, you need to understand one more thing: You can leave this prison.

I left mine. Hundreds of people I have mentored left theirs. You can leave yours, too.

Let's move forward.

POINTS TO REMEMBER

If you take nothing else from this chapter, take this: distraction is not primarily a virtue problem. It is not proof that you are weak, lazy, or defective. It is far more often the predictable result of a nervous system living in an environment that constantly provokes craving and stress. When you understand that, shame begins to loosen its grip, and you can finally address the real issue instead of attacking yourself.

Your attention is shaped by chemistry. Dopamine drives the urge to seek—always reaching for the next hit of novelty, the next reward, the next quick relief. Cortisol keeps your body braced for threat, and a braced body does not focus well because it is scanning for danger, not settling into depth. When these two chemicals begin to feed each other, people get trapped in a loop: stress drives seeking, seeking fragments the mind, fragmentation creates more stress. It feels like a discipline problem, but it behaves like biology.

The way out is not perfection and it is not willpower alone. You cannot out-discipline a deregulated nervous system. You cannot shame yourself into steadiness. What you can do is learn to regulate—to choose practices that restore the chemistry of clarity, presence, and connection. The PRECEPT Framework is built for that kind of return: not to fix who you are, but to restore the internal conditions that make you fully human again.

And remember this, especially if you feel discouraged: what is buried is not destroyed. Your focus, your peace, your wisdom, your ability to lead from steadiness—those things are still there. They have simply been crowded out by noise and hijacked chemistry. When the chemistry begins to change, the person you remember begins to reappear.

CHAPTER 3

Why "Trying Harder" Doesn't Work

A Story to Start: "Day Eight"

There is a particular kind of confidence that shows up right before a relapse. It's not loud confidence. It's quiet, private confidence—the kind you don't announce because you don't want anyone watching in case you fail. It's the confidence that whispers, *This time will be different. I've learned my lesson. I've paid enough consequences. I've got it under control.*

For me, that confidence often arrived around day six or day seven. Seven days without a drink. Seven days without cocaine. Seven days of white-knuckling it and telling myself I had proven something. I could feel pride rising like a shield: *See? You can do this. The whole thing has been exaggerated. You're fine.*

And then something would happen that addicts understand better than most people.

Everyone wants a trigger. We all want to believe relapse is logical—like a code you can crack if you just find the right cause. *If I can identify the one thing that sets me off, I'll be safe.* So you search for patterns: stress at work, a fight at home, a bad day, a lonely night. And yes, sometimes life throws a clear punch. Sometimes it hurts, and you reach for relief.

But here's what I learned the hard way: the "trigger" isn't reliable.

You can be happy and relapse. You can be sad and relapse. You can be melancholic, bored, anxious, restless, or completely neutral and relapse. You can have a great day and still find yourself driving toward the same old escape as if your hands are on a steering wheel your mind isn't fully holding.

That's what makes addiction so terrifying. The relapse doesn't always begin with pain. It begins with a shift—an internal click—like a trapdoor opening beneath your logic. It's as if a different part of you takes the microphone. The rational part that made the promises doesn't disappear, but it goes quiet. And the craving part starts speaking with authority.

It doesn't come in shouting, *I'm here to destroy your life.*

It comes in sounding reasonable. Familiar. Even deserved.

You deserve relief.

And once that argument lands, it's off to the races. The insanity takes over. The binge begins. The cycle starts again—not because you planned it, but because something in you has been trained to run that path the moment the gate opens.

For me, day eight was the line I couldn't seem to cross. I'd make it to seven days and then collapse back into the old pattern, and every collapse trained me to believe the same lie: *Next time I'll try harder.* But eight days carried a different weight. I hadn't gone eight days without a drink since high school. Eight days felt impossible. Eight days wasn't just progress—it was a boundary.

And here's the part that still feels like grace when I look back: once I got to eight days, I never went back.

That's why I'm careful when people talk about addiction—or distraction—as if the solution is simply stronger effort. Because if effort alone were enough, day eight would have been easy. I wanted sobriety. I feared what I was becoming. I had reasons to stop. I had promises. I had consequences. But those things didn't automatically translate into freedom. Something deeper had to change.

■　■　■　■

There came a point in my life when everything around me was screaming, "You have a problem." Finances were collapsing. My health was declining. Relationships were crumbling. Jobs disappeared as fast as opportunities arrived. And still, I told myself the same lie most addicts tell: *I've got this under control.*

When you're addicted—to alcohol, to drugs, to screens—it's amazing how creative the mind becomes at explaining away the truth. I justified every bad outcome with a reason that kept me safe from reality. "That deal fell through because the market shifted." "I drink because work is stressful." "Everyone unwinds somehow." The explanations were flexible enough to cover any evidence and strong enough to protect me from the one conclusion I didn't want to face.

Meanwhile, something else was happening that I didn't understand at the time. The good influences—the grounded people, the steady ones, the ones who carried peace with them—began to drift away. Not because they were cruel, but because health doesn't thrive in environments built around denial. And the ones who stayed were almost always the ones trapped in the same self-destruction I was. Misery doesn't just love company; it depends on it. It needs a crowd to normalize the madness.

Then came the small crack in my logic: *Maybe I'm drinking a little too much.*

That thought terrified me because if it was true, it meant something worse might also be true: *Maybe I can't stop.*

The Myth of Control

For a long time I believed I could quit whenever I wanted. And sometimes I did—at least for a few days. I'd make it a week. Seven days of white-knuckling it. Seven days of pride, followed by one night of surrender.

Every relapse strengthened the same strategy: next time I would just try harder.

That's what our culture teaches, isn't it? That discipline fixes everything. That the answer to every struggle is more effort, more grit, more self-control. If something is broken, tighten your grip.

But discipline can't override chemistry.

My problem wasn't a lack of effort; it was a brain hijacked by dopamine. Alcohol and cocaine flood the brain with dopamine—the chemical that doesn't simply say, "That felt good." It says, "That felt necessary. Do it again." Each time I drank or used, that chemical surge trained my brain to crave the next hit. The craving wasn't an idea. It was a demand.

Then tolerance moved in. I needed more to feel the same. What used to be a rush eventually became normal, and what used to feel normal eventually felt like withdrawal. The entire system kept shifting until I wasn't chasing pleasure anymore—I was chasing relief.

Why Willpower Fails

Most people think willpower is like a muscle: strengthen it and you'll be able to resist anything. But willpower behaves less like a muscle and more like a battery. It drains quickly.

Every time you resist temptation—whether it's a drink, a donut, or the dopamine hit of social media—you burn energy. You are not simply making a choice; you are fighting your own chemistry. And eventually that chemistry wins, not because you are weak, but because biology is persistent.

Neuroscientists describe a tension between the part of your brain that helps you plan, delay gratification, and choose what matters over what feels good right now, and older systems that govern survival and reward. The prefrontal cortex is where intentions live; it's where you make promises, set goals, and imagine a better future. But the limbic system is older, faster, and less interested in your plans. When it senses reward—or when it senses that relief is available—it can override logic.

THE UNCOMFORTABLE TRUTH

If your plan for change is "try harder," you don't have a plan yet. You have a wish.

It doesn't ask whether the choice aligns with your values. It asks whether the choice promises relief.

That is why "trying harder" rarely works for long. Willpower is fighting biology. And biology, given enough time, usually gets what it wants.

Fast Dopamine Vs. Slow Dopamine

The modern world runs on fast dopamine—quick hits of pleasure and instant feedback. We don't have to wait for much anymore. And waiting, inconvenient as it feels, is one of the ways a person becomes steady. Waiting develops patience. Waiting builds tolerance. Waiting teaches the nervous system how to hold discomfort without panicking.

Fast dopamine skips all of that. It delivers reward without effort, relief without process, stimulation without meaning.

For me, alcohol and cocaine were the fast dopamine of my twenties. For many people today, fast dopamine looks different: social media, news cycles, YouTube, video games, online shopping, endless email loops. The substances change, but the circuitry is familiar.

Fast dopamine feels good now. Slow dopamine feels good later. Fast dopamine gives you a rush; slow dopamine gives you meaning.

You get fast dopamine from scrolling. You get slow dopamine from reading. You get fast dopamine from checking likes; slow dopamine from building a relationship. Fast dopamine from consuming; slow dopamine from creating. Fast dopamine from reaction; slow dopamine from reflection.

Fast dopamine is like sugar: a little won't kill you, but binging all day will rot your peace from the inside out. It trains your brain to expect constant reward and then punishes you with restlessness when the reward isn't available.

The Turning Point

When I finally stopped drinking, I didn't do it through willpower. I did it through substitution.

Instead of going to a bar after work, I went to an AA meeting. Instead of staying out until 2 a.m., I went to Blockbuster with my dad and picked two movies for the weekend. Later I watched them with a friend—then with Barb, who became my wife of thirty-three years.

Those nights weren't about the movies. They were about replacement. They were about building a new rhythm of life—one hour at a time. I wasn't merely saying no to something destructive. I was learning how to say yes to something steady, something connecting, something real.

That's what freedom looks like in real time. Not heroic resistance. Not dramatic transformation. A better pattern, practiced until it becomes normal.

From Addiction to Distraction

Fast forward a few decades. The bar is gone, but the pull is still there.

Now it's my phone. It's the endless loop of YouTube clips, Instagram reels, Facebook scrolls—each one a miniature dopamine drip. It's the same voice whispering, "Just one more." And I can justify it just as easily as I used to justify drinking.

"I'm watching something educational."

"I'm catching up on industry news."

"I'm researching."

Deep down, I know what's happening. I'm not drinking anymore—but I'm still feeding the same circuitry.

The difference is that alcohol destroyed my body. Screens destroy my focus. Both rob time. Both numb pain. Both promise connection and deliver emptiness if you live there long enough.

The Real Problem Isn't Screens—It's Substitution

We think the problem is the device. But the deeper problem is what the device replaces.

When we scroll, we don't merely waste time—we substitute meaning. We scroll instead of praying. We binge instead of reading. We react instead of reflecting. We consume instead of creating. Over time, the screen doesn't simply take minutes; it takes the practices that build identity.

This is why the opposite of addiction isn't sobriety. The opposite of addiction is connection.

That is what the **PRECEPT Framework** is built around—reconnection. Each discipline—**Pray, Read, Exercise, Capture, Engage, Practice, Think**—is a way to replace fast dopamine with slow dopamine, to move from consumption to creation, from reaction to reflection.

Why "Trying Harder" Fails and Replacing Works

Here's what I've learned over nearly four decades of sobriety: you can't fight your biology—you have to rewire it.

Rewiring doesn't start with grand resolutions. It starts small.

When I got sober, people told me not to worry about staying sober forever—just for one day. I couldn't imagine a lifetime without alcohol, but I could make it twenty-four hours. Then twenty-four hours became a week, a month, a year, a life.

That's how recovery works: one day at a time, one choice at a time, one substitution at a time.

It's the same with distraction. You don't have to delete every app or throw your phone in a lake. You have to start small—replace one destructive loop with one constructive practice.

Read instead of scroll. Pray instead of post. Capture instead of consume. Do that once, then again tomorrow.

That's how you build new chemistry, new habits, and a new life.

A Different Kind of Discipline

This is the great irony: freedom requires structure.

You don't need more discipline. You need a different kind—built on design, not denial.

When I first got sober, I didn't rely on willpower. I relied on systems: meetings, accountability, and a spiritual foundation. When I began facing digital distraction, I did the same thing. I built structure around focus, reflection, and rest, because I had learned the hard way that good intentions are not enough when the nervous system is hungry.

The PRECEPT Framework isn't about restriction. It's about redirection.

You're not unplugging from life. You're plugging back into it.

The answer isn't trying harder. It's replacing faster—replacing habits that numb with habits that nourish, replacing reaction with reflection, replacing chaos with calm.

Because in the end, you don't need a stronger will.

You need a better way.

POINTS TO REMEMBER

If you have been stuck in the cycle of promising yourself you'll change and then watching yourself repeat the same pattern, you are not alone—and you are not uniquely broken. The most important thing to remember is that "trying harder" fails for a reason. It fails because willpower is not designed to overpower a hijacked reward system for very long. You can mean well and still lose the fight, not because you lack character, but because your nervous system is running a script it has rehearsed thousands of times.

Addiction—and modern distraction—thrives in the myth of control. It convinces you that next time you'll manage it, regulate it, limit it, or stop it through sheer effort. But when chemistry drives behavior, effort alone becomes a temporary dam against a powerful current. Eventually the current finds a crack. The relapse doesn't always require a dramatic trigger, either. You can be happy, sad, bored, anxious, or neutral and still watch the insanity take the wheel. That unpredictability isn't proof that you're hopeless; it's proof that your brain has learned a pattern that activates on its own.

The way out is not heroic resistance; it is purposeful replacement. Freedom is built less by saying "no" to the old life and more by creating a better one—one substitution at a time. Fast dopamine offers immediate relief and long-term regret. Slow dopamine offers delayed reward and deep meaning. The PRECEPT Framework is designed to move you steadily from fast dopamine to slow dopamine, from reaction to reflection, from consumption to creation, and from isolation to connection.

Finally, remember that structure is not the enemy of freedom. It is the path to it. When you build systems that support who you are becoming—practices that regulate your nervous system instead of inflaming it—you stop relying on willpower as your only tool. You begin rewiring the circuitry itself. That is how day one becomes day eight, and day eight becomes a life you don't want to escape from anymore.

CHAPTER 4

The Turning Point

When the Fast Became a Framework

A STORY TO START: "THE AUDITORIUM."

The auditorium was packed that morning—hundreds of people, lights, music, screens, the kind of energy you can feel in your chest before you even sit down. Barb and I found seats about halfway back. The room buzzed with anticipation, and I could tell we weren't the only ones who had come hungry for something we didn't quite know how to name.

Darren Whitehead was speaking. People had been talking about it for weeks. Darren had written *The Digital Fast*, and the whole thing had that feeling of a moment—like we were walking into a conversation that had already started in the culture and was finally catching up with our personal lives.

I didn't come out of curiosity. I came because I knew I needed this.

For months, I'd felt that familiar pull again—the creeping drift that starts when you're telling yourself you're fine but deep down you know something's off. Not alcohol this time. Not the kind of addiction that leaves bottles behind and consequences you can't hide.

This one was quieter. More respectable.

This one fit in my pocket.

The Message That Hit Home

Darren walked on stage with an easy grin, his Australian accent cutting through the noise like a blade through cloth. He opened with humor, telling stories about his kids and how they loved to tease him about being "from the 1900s." The room laughed with him. It was light, disarming, the way good speakers can lower a guard without making you feel manipulated.

Then he shifted the atmosphere with a story that wasn't dramatic at all, which is probably why it worked.

He told us about taking his daughters out on one-on-one dates. He would ask them the kind of question that good parents ask because they're brave enough to want honest answers. "What's Dad doing right that he should do more of?" he asked them. Their answers were sweet and predictable. They talked about being present, being fun, being kind. The kinds of affirmations that warm you.

Then he asked the other question. The one that takes courage to ask.

"What's Dad doing wrong?"

And he said every one of his daughters gave him the same answer: "I wish you weren't always on your phone."

Those words sank into me like a stone.

I glanced around the room, and you could feel what happened. Hundreds of people suddenly still, like the air itself had tightened. No one moved. No one coughed. It wasn't guilt, exactly. It was recognition. We all knew exactly what he meant.

Then Darren read from 1 Peter 5:8: "Be alert and of sober mind. Your enemy, the devil, prowls around like a roaring lion looking for someone to devour."

It was a verse I had heard before. I knew it. But that morning it landed differently, not as a warning for somebody else, but as a mirror held up close.

"Be alert," he said again. "Be awake. Be clearheaded."

Then he talked about how the thief doesn't steal everything all at once. He takes a little here, a little there—time, presence, peace—until one day you look up and realize you've been robbed without ever hearing the door break down. Darren used the word *klepto*, from the Greek: to steal without you noticing.

And I thought, *That's exactly what's been happening to me.*

The Wake-Up

As Darren spoke, he showed a timeline—a visual of how people spend their time from 1930 to now. Family and friendship used to dominate. Church used to be near the top. Then, decade by decade, as technology crept in, those bars shrank. By 2024, he said, 61% of our waking hours would be spent in front of screens.

He shared numbers about phone use—five to six hours a day for the average adult, seven to nine for teenagers. Then he said the average attention span had dropped to eight seconds, a second less than a goldfish.

People laughed, but I didn't.

It wasn't because the statistic offended me. It was because I could see myself inside it. Another man whose days disappeared into the bright glow of screens. Another leader, another husband, another father, convincing himself that his scrolling was "work," that his constant checking was "staying informed," that his digital intake was an unavoidable part of modern life.

Darren asked the question that sealed it for me: "We use our phones to control our lives, but what if they're controlling us?"

That's when it clicked.

Not in a dramatic moment, but in the way truth clicks when it has been circling you for months and finally lands. My clarity, my presence, my focus—numbed by a thousand digital sips a day. Not the kind of numbness that makes you fall over, but the kind that makes you forget what it feels like to be fully awake.

The 28-day Digital Fast

When Darren invited the church to join a 28-day digital fast, I was in before he finished the sentence. I bought the workbook. I made the decision with the kind of urgency that usually means you have finally stopped negotiating with yourself.

I didn't want to simply subtract. I wanted to substitute.

I had learned, decades earlier, that you can't build a new life out of empty space. If you remove something that has been functioning as relief, you have to replace it with something richer—or the old thing will come back with a louder voice.

So I made a plan. I decided that the time I had been giving to screens would be given to things that nourished me instead of numbed me. I would walk. I would play guitar. I'd practice bass or piano. I would build a small corner in the house for creativity—an analog sanctuary. I would read more. Think more. Be present.

And for the first few days it worked. The noise quieted. I wasn't checking my phone at night. I wasn't flipping on the TV after dinner. The silence felt uncomfortable at first, like a room you haven't entered in a long time. But then, slowly, the discomfort began to soften into something else.

Peace.

The Crack in the Armor

But by the end of the first week, the same old voice came whispering back.

"Just an hour of news. It's good to stay informed."

"Just check your podcast analytics. That's work."

I justified it all so easily. After all, I wasn't drinking. I wasn't gambling. I wasn't hurting anyone. I was just... checking.

But the pattern was identical to the one I had lived decades before. A subtle slide from intention to rationalization, from clarity to compromise. And like addiction, it happens in silence, where no one confronts you and you can keep telling yourself whatever story protects you.

By the end of the 28 days, the games were back. The social media apps had snuck onto my phone again. I told myself I was doing better—and I was, technically—but I knew in my gut I hadn't solved the problem.

A fast can interrupt a pattern.

But interruption is not the same as transformation.

Friday Nights and Waiting Rooms

Friday became the mirror again. Every week I would sit down exhausted but restless and think, *What happened to my time?* It wasn't that I hadn't worked. It was that I had worked without focus—every task interrupted, every margin filled, every quiet moment taken before it could become anything sacred.

At the same time, I was caring for my eighty-nine-year-old dad, sitting for hours in hospital and VA waiting rooms. And everywhere I looked, I saw the same posture: heads bowed to screens.

Not one or two. Everyone.

No eye contact. No conversation. No impatience that led to human connection. Just the silent glow. It was like a public ritual we had all agreed not to name. A quiet captivity disguised as normal.

As I watched, Darren's words echoed: "The thief comes to steal, kill, and destroy."

What was being stolen wasn't merely time. It was our capacity to think, to feel, to be still long enough to remember what matters. It was our ability to be quiet enough to hear God's voice.

Counting Minutes

One night I sat at my desk and did the math.

There are 10,080 minutes in a week.

When I counted honestly, I realized I was spending more than 4,000 of those minutes in front of screens. Not all wasted. Some productive. But much of it not purposeful—minutes that didn't build anything in me, minutes that didn't deepen relationships, minutes that didn't move me toward the man I wanted to become.

An old saying floated up: "Count your pennies, and the dollars will come."

Maybe it was time to start counting minutes.

Because minutes become hours, hours become days, and days become weeks. And if I didn't reclaim those minutes, I would lose more than time.

I would lose meaning.

THE ACCOUNTING THAT MATTERS

There are 10,080 minutes in a week. If you don't decide where they go, something else will.

From Limiting to Replacing

That night something old but familiar stirred in me—the memory of early sobriety.

When I quit drinking in 1989, I didn't do it by sheer willpower. I did it through replacement. Instead of going to bars, I went to meetings. Instead of wasting nights alone, I watched movies with my dad. Later those movies became time with Barb, who would become my wife of thirty-three years.

Recovery taught me that transformation doesn't happen through restriction. It happens through substitution. And suddenly the principle felt obvious: the same thing applied here.

I didn't need to simply "quit screens." I needed to replace the role screens were playing in my life. I needed to replace fast dopamine with slow dopamine, numbness with nourishment, reaction with reflection. I needed a way to answer the real question that was underneath the whole struggle.

How do I cope?

In early sobriety, "coping" was not a slogan. It was survival. Coping meant learning how to live inside my own skin without reaching for the old anesthetic. It meant having something ready for the moment the craving showed up—something simple, something practical, something available at the exact moment the temptation tried to negotiate.

So I began writing down replacements—small actions that could interrupt the loop and turn me back toward life. Four of them came quickly, and they formed a plain, honest acronym that made me smile when it appeared on the page:

C.O.P.E.

- **Create something.** Not because it had to be impressive, but because creation pulls you out of consumption and reminds you that you are more than a receptacle for information.
- **Organize something.** A drawer, a desk, a schedule, a corner of the garage—anything that restores a sense of order, because chaos outside often mirrors chaos within.
- **Practice something.** A scale on the guitar, a skill you've neglected, a craft you once loved—practice returns you to patience and builds slow dopamine the honest way.
- **Exercise something.** A walk, a stretch, movement of any kind—because the body cannot carry stress indefinitely without paying a price.

C.O.P.E. was a great start, but it wasn't complete.

It helped me interrupt the craving. It helped me redirect energy. It helped me move, instead of spiral. But as the days went on, I realized I wasn't only battling distraction. I was battling disconnection. And disconnection isn't solved by activity alone. It's solved by returning to the deeper practices that rebuild the inner life—practices that don't just occupy time, but restore meaning.

So I kept refining. I kept praying and thinking. I added what I knew my soul actually needed, not just what my restless brain would tolerate.

"Pray," I wrote, because what I needed wasn't merely calm; I needed alignment.

"Read," because my mind had been trained for fragments and I needed depth again.

"Think," because wisdom doesn't form when you're constantly reacting.

"Engage," because the opposite of addiction isn't sobriety—it's connection.

Slowly a word emerged, like a shape coming into focus.

PRECEPT.

The Birth of PRECEPT

PRECEPT wasn't born as an idea. It was born as a lifeline.

It wasn't theory. It was survival.

A simple way to redirect my energy when distraction tried to pull me back under. Each letter became a rhythm, a discipline, a kind of spiritual training:

Pray. Read. Exercise. Capture. Engage. Practice. Think.

Each one became a substitute for scrolling, zoning out, being pulled into the vortex of fast dopamine. Each one became a way to return from fragmentation to wholeness.

And it worked.

Not perfectly. Not every day. But slowly my time began to take shape again. My attention stopped feeling like a leaking bucket. My evenings became less restless. My mind became quieter. Not because life got easier, but because my inner world began to stabilize.

The point wasn't to delete screens.

It was to design a life worth living without them.

The Real Digital Fast

Looking back on that Sunday in the auditorium, I realized the digital fast wasn't really about technology. It was about attention—where it goes and what it grows.

Darren's challenge wasn't simply about deleting apps. It was about rediscovering presence. He said something that stayed with me: the digital fast is not only a call to put something down; it's a call to pick something up.

That's what PRECEPT became for me.

It became my way of picking up the right things again—habits that reconnect me to God, to people, and to purpose. And the surprising thing was that when I finally put down my phone, I didn't feel empty.

I felt awake.

And that's when the real conversation with God began again.

POINTS TO REMEMBER

Turning points rarely arrive as lightning. Most of the time they arrive as recognition—one sentence that lands, one question that won't leave you alone, one moment when you can no longer pretend you don't know what you know. A crowded auditorium became my mirror, but the real turning point followed me into ordinary life: into Friday nights when my time felt stolen, into waiting rooms where an entire culture sat quietly medicating itself, into the moment I counted minutes and realized how much of my week was being given away.

A fast can interrupt a pattern, but interruption is not the same as transformation. If you only subtract, the empty space will eventually be filled again—often by the very thing you tried to remove. That is why replacement matters. And that is why C.O.P.E. mattered. It gave me handles—simple actions I could take when the pull showed up. It was a way to answer the urgent question underneath temptation: *How do I cope right now without going back to the old prison?*

But coping is only the beginning. If you stop at coping, you may reduce damage, but you won't necessarily rebuild depth. Over time, I realized I needed more than interruption; I needed reconnection. I needed practices that didn't merely keep my hands busy, but restored my mind, my relationships, and my ability to hear God in the quiet.

That is what kept unfolding into PRECEPT—Pray, Read, Exercise, Capture, Engage, Practice, Think—not as a clever concept, but as a path back to wholeness. The goal was never to become a person who never touches a screen. The goal was to become a person with a life so full of meaning that screens no longer function as my primary source of relief.

And that is the real turning point: when you stop trying to manage the thief and start rebuilding what was stolen.

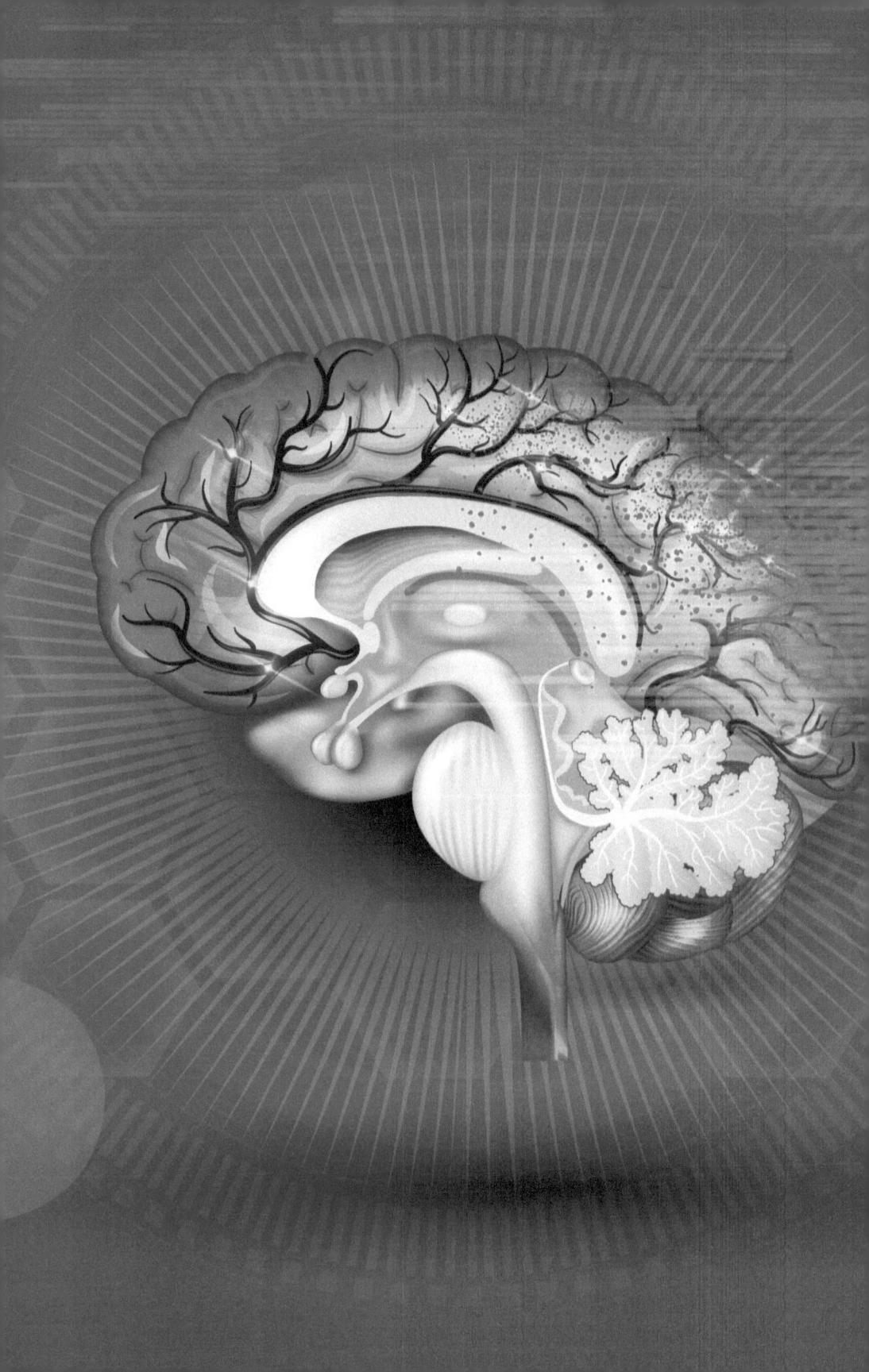

PART II

THE PRECEPT
Framework

CHAPTER 5

Why PRECEPT?
(The Word, the Math, the Meaning)

A Story to Start: "Day Tripper"

It happened in the space between things.

No crisis. No bad news. No urgent call. Just a quiet pause—one of those small gaps that show up all day long and feel strangely empty if you don't know what to do with them. I was standing in the kitchen, waiting for coffee, and my hand drifted toward my phone the way it always does. Not because I needed something, but because my nervous system wanted something. A little stimulation. A little relief. A little novelty to smooth out the silence.

That's what makes distraction so difficult to fight. It rarely comes as a bold temptation. It comes as a reflex. It comes as a whisper: *Just check for a second*. It comes disguised as harmless.

My thumb hovered, and I felt the current begin—the subtle slide from intention to autopilot. I knew where it would go if I let it. I'd open a feed, skim a headline, watch a clip, follow a link, and look up later with that familiar feeling: *I was just there, but I wasn't really there.*

So instead of feeding it, I turned.

In our house my guitars aren't tucked away in cases. They're hung on the wall, right out in the open—an invitation and a reminder. I own several. Each one holds a different voice in the wood, a different feel under the fingers, a different kind of memory. I walked over and reached for my Taylor.

The moment I lifted it off the wall, something shifted in me. My shoulders dropped a fraction. My breathing slowed. The instrument had weight—real weight—in my hands, and that alone brought me back into the physical world. I sat down and started playing an old Beatles tune, "Day Tripper."

I've always been fascinated by what's happening inside a musician's brain when they play. It isn't a single-track experience. Your hands are doing one thing while your ears are monitoring tone and timing. Your mind is anticipating the next chord change. Your body is keeping rhythm. Emotion is involved, memory is involved, and meaning is involved. When you play, you're not consuming. You're participating. Your whole brain shows up.

And as I fell into the song, something else happened—the kind of thing that never happens when I'm scrolling. The lyrics came forward.

There's a line in that song that talks about being teased—pulled by something that promises satisfaction but doesn't deliver it. Only this time I wasn't thinking about a person in a story. I was thinking about the lure I carry in my pocket. That quick digital hit that feels like it might finally land, might finally satisfy, might finally settle the itch. And yet it never does. It gives you a taste and leaves you wanting. It offers you relief and then quietly hands you restlessness. It takes you "half the way," and then it strands you there—still reaching, still hungry, still not full.

Sitting there with the Taylor on my lap, the connection felt almost too perfect to ignore. The song became a mirror. I could see the pattern: the tease of fast dopamine, the promise of the next swipe, the next clip, the next little hit that never becomes enough.

That moment—phone in one direction, guitar in the other—wasn't about music. It was about identity. It was proof that I could still choose what restores me. It was proof that the thief doesn't get the next minute automatically.

And it reminded me of something I'm going to come back to again and again in this part of the book: if you don't choose your life before the moment arrives, the moment will choose for you.

■　■　■　■

Part I named the war for our attention. We explored the drift—how people lose themselves slowly, not through catastrophe but through erosion. We talked about brain chemistry and the way dopamine and cortisol work together to keep people compulsively reaching for relief. We told the truth about why "trying harder" doesn't work when your nervous system is hijacked. And we ended with a turning point—the moment I realized I couldn't simply delete a few apps and hope for a different life. I needed replacement. I needed structure. I needed a path.

Part II is that path.

And it begins with a simple question that carries more weight than it seems: why call this framework PRECEPT?

Why the Word Matters

Words shape how we think. And how we think shapes what we attempt.

If I called this a productivity system, you'd assume the goal is efficiency—doing more, moving faster, squeezing outcomes out of your days. But efficiency is not what most people are craving. Most people aren't exhausted because they aren't organized. They're exhausted because they are fragmented. They don't need to become faster. They need to become whole.

If I called this a digital detox, you might assume the goal is to get away from technology. But technology isn't the only thief. A person can be distracted without a phone. The deeper issue is attention—where it goes and what it grows. This is not ultimately a technology problem.

It's a formation problem.

PRECEPT is the right word because it points to something deeper than tactics. It points to the power of a guiding principle chosen ahead of time—before the moment arrives.

The Etymology of "Precept": Guidance Chosen in Advance

The word *precept* carries an old, sturdy meaning: instruction or guidance given beforehand. A precept is not something you invent under pressure. It is something you choose while you are clearheaded, sober-minded, and awake.

That "beforehand" quality is the key.

Most people try to change in the worst possible place: inside the moment of temptation. They wait until they are tired, stressed, lonely, bored, or wired on cortisol, and then they attempt to improvise a better response in real time. That is like waiting until you're already in a storm to decide whether you believe in anchors.

A precept is an anchor dropped before the storm.

It is roofing built on a clear day.

It is a boundary drawn before you reach the edge.

This is why the Scripture Darren read struck me: "Be alert and of sober mind."

WHY PRECEPTS WORK

In the moment, you don't choose from wisdom. You choose from appetite. A precept is wisdom chosen ahead of time—so you can live it later.

Alertness is the posture in which you choose a precept. You choose it when you're awake enough to tell the truth. You choose it when you can see the pattern clearly and decide what you will do the next time the pattern tries to pull you under.

And because the thief steals quietly—not in dramatic collapses but in small compromises—the response has to be quietly intentional. Not performative. Not frantic. A precept is the kind of guidance that can survive ordinary life.

It helps you decide in advance what you will do when your body wants relief and your mind wants escape. It gives you something sturdier than a mood. It gives you a plan that doesn't depend on you feeling strong that day.

Precepts Vs. Rules: Why This Isn't Legalism

When some people hear the word "precept," they hear *rule*. They picture finger-wagging, restriction, spiritual performance, or a new checklist they will eventually fail.

That is not what I mean.

Rules are often imposed from the outside. Precepts are chosen from the inside.

Rules can create image management—looking good while staying unchanged. Precepts create formation—becoming steady even when no one is watching.

Rules are often about earning something. Precepts are about protecting something.

And what we are protecting here is not a reputation. We are protecting your attention, your clarity, your ability to be present with your life and with God. We are protecting the inner conditions where wisdom can form.

If you've ever tried to change through sheer restriction, you know what happens. You last for a while, then you break. Not because you're hopeless, but because restriction without replacement creates a vacuum. The old habit comes back to fill the space because it was serving a purpose—regulating stress, numbing pain, providing relief.

PRECEPT is not primarily about restriction. It is about replacement and restoration. It isn't designed to make your life smaller.

It's designed to make it deeper.

The Math Idea You Didn't Expect: Procept

There's another reason PRECEPT fits, and it surprised me when I first saw it.

In math education, there is an idea called a *procept*—a symbol that is both a process and the result of that process. Early on, an expression like "3 + 2" is a process: you do something. Over time, it becomes an object: you immediately know the result. The symbol holds both realities—the action and the outcome.

That idea is one of the best metaphors I've ever found for transformation.

In the beginning, PRECEPT is a process. It is something you do. You pray when you want to scroll. You read when your brain wants quick hits. You exercise when stress is building. You capture thoughts instead of letting your mind spin. You engage with people instead of escaping into screens. You practice skills instead of consuming content. You think instead of reacting.

At first, those practices feel like effort because you are building something new.

But over time, PRECEPT becomes more than a set of actions.

It becomes the result of those actions.

It becomes the kind of person you are.

This is where most people misunderstand habit change. They think habits are about behavior management. They don't realize habits are about identity formation. What you repeatedly practice doesn't just change what you do; it changes what you desire. It changes what feels normal. It changes what you reach for when you are stressed.

PRECEPT starts as a discipline.

Then it becomes an identity.

PRECEPT becomes both a discipline you practice and a person you become.

The Framework as a Trellis

Some people hear "framework" and assume restriction. Something rigid. Something heavy. Something that will make life smaller.

But PRECEPT isn't a cage. It's a trellis.

A trellis doesn't restrict a vine because it dislikes the vine. A trellis gives a vine structure so it can grow upward instead of collapsing under its own weight. Without structure, the vine spreads everywhere and produces less fruit. With structure, it becomes healthier, stronger, more fruitful.

That's what PRECEPT provides: structure that creates freedom. Not rules to impress people. Rhythms that restore you.

The goal of this book is not for you to become somebody who never touches a screen. The goal is for you to become somebody with enough inner steadiness that screens no longer function as your primary source of relief. The goal is presence. Clarity. Depth. Wisdom. A life you don't need to escape from.

Where We Go From Here

The reason I begin Part II with the word PRECEPT is simple: this is not a collection of tips. It is not inspiration you admire and forget. It is a framework designed to be lived. It is guidance chosen ahead of time so you can live with clarity when the moment comes for you again—when you're tired, when you're stressed, when you're lonely, when the phone calls to you like a quick exit.

In the chapters ahead, we will walk through each letter. We will move slowly and practically, because the work we're doing is not performance. It is formation. You will not change all at once, because that isn't how people change. But you can change steadily. And steady change, over time, is how a life comes back.

POINTS TO REMEMBER

Most change fails because it is attempted too late. People wait until they are tired, tempted, stressed, or lonely and then try to improvise a better life in real time. A precept is guidance chosen beforehand—an anchored principle you decide on while you are clearheaded, so you can live by it when your nervous system is loud.

PRECEPT is not a legalistic list of rules. Rules are often imposed from the outside and can create performance. Precepts are chosen from the inside and create formation. This framework is not about restriction for its own sake; it is about replacement and restoration—rebuilding the inner rhythms that screens and modern busyness have pushed aside.

PRECEPT is also both a process and a result. Like the mathematical idea of a procept, it starts as something you do and becomes something you are. In the beginning you practice the disciplines. Over time, the disciplines shape you—your attention, your identity, and your ability to live awake.

A Note to the Skeptical Reader

I need to say something before we go any further, because the first letter of PRECEPT is going to land differently depending on what you've lived through. For some of you, prayer will feel familiar—like home. For others, it will feel like a word you've spent years avoiding. And if you're in that second group, I want you to hear this clearly: I'm not here to corner you, shame you, or win an argument.

Some of you were taught that faith is naïve and prayer is a crutch—something the weak lean on because they can't face reality. Others didn't need a professor to turn you away. You were turned away by people. By hypocrisy. By religious pressure that felt more like control than love. Maybe you grew up with a version of God that sounded harsh, disappointed, and impossible to please. Or maybe you tried praying when you were hurting and you heard nothing back, and silence became your conclusion.

If that's you, you're not crazy for feeling resistant. You're not defective. You're not "too far gone." You're human. And I'm not asking you to manufacture belief you don't have.

What I am asking for—at least at the beginning—is something much smaller and much more honest.

Willingness.

Not willingness to agree with me. Not willingness to join a religion. Just willingness to consider that you might not be able to think your way out of everything you feel. Willingness to consider that the ache inside you isn't just intellectual—it's personal. It's relational. It's spiritual. And that the life you want—clarity, peace, joy, steadiness—may require help that doesn't originate inside your own willpower.

If you've ever sat in a class where God was treated like a superstition and faith was dismissed as a psychological coping mechanism, you can still be a serious thinker and admit this: your mind is not the only part of you that matters. You have a nervous system. You have a heart. You have loneliness and longing and fear and shame and hope. You have questions that logic alone doesn't quiet at two in the morning.

And here's the quiet irony: the very posture your culture praises—self-sufficiency—can become its own prison. Because when you're hurting, and you're alone with your mind, and you've told yourself there's no one to call on but you, you are forced to carry a weight humans weren't designed to carry.

That's why prayer matters in this framework.

Prayer is not pretending you're certain. Prayer is not performing religion. Prayer is not closing your eyes and denying reality. Prayer is turning toward reality with honesty and saying, even if you can barely whisper it, "I need help."

If that's all you can do right now, that's enough. Start there.

And if you're a parent who handed this book to a son or daughter because you can see they're hurting, I want to tell you something too: you don't have to force this. You don't have to argue them into God. You don't have to win debates to heal a heart. The goal here isn't to pressure anyone into belief. The goal is to open a door that pain has already cracked—gently, patiently, without coercion—so they can step toward life again.

Jesus once said, "The thief comes only to steal and kill and destroy; I have come that they may have life, and have it to the full." Whether you trust that sentence yet or not, you probably recognize the first half. You've felt the stealing. The thinning. The quiet loss of joy. What we're doing now is moving toward the second half—toward life.

So if prayer feels loaded, start simple. Start honest. Start with the only thing you might be able to say without pretending:

"God... if You're there... help me."

CHAPTER 6

PRAY: Connection Before Action

A Story to Start: "How Do You Pray?"

Over the last almost four decades, I've sat in more recovery meetings than I could count. Different rooms. Different churches. Different basements. Different coffee. Same honesty. Same desperation. Same quiet courage.

And one question comes up again and again—usually not from the people who have been around for years, but from the ones who are new. The ones who are walking in with shaking hands and an exhausted face and a life that has finally become unmanageable.

They don't come in because life is going so well. They come in because they're broken. They're at the end of their rope. They've tried every version of self-control they know. They've tried making deals with themselves. They've tried promises. They've tried willpower. They've tried shame, too—because shame is the tool many of us reach for when we don't know what else to do.

And when you're new, you hear people talk about prayer. A lot. You hear things like "turn it over," and "let go," and "ask God for help." You hear sayings like, "There aren't any atheists in foxholes."

Most newcomers understand the foxhole prayer immediately. They already know how to pray when the fear is big enough.

It usually sounds something like: *God, if You're up there... please help.*

Most people have that down.

But eventually, once the immediate crisis quiets a little, they start noticing something else. They notice people who aren't just surviving. They notice people who have steadiness. They notice a kind of calm that doesn't seem fake. They notice men and women who can tell the truth without collapsing under it, who can face consequences without spiraling, who can live through pain without reaching for the old anesthetic.

And then the question comes—the more honest, less dramatic, deeply human question:

"How do you pray?"

Not "Do you pray?" but "How?"

Because in that moment, they're not asking about religion. They're asking about relationship. They're asking about access. They're asking how to reach for something real instead of another temporary fix.

That question matters in this book for a simple reason: distraction is not chemical dependence in the same way alcohol or drugs are. A screen won't destroy your liver. Infinite scroll won't put you in jail. You can hold down a job while being quietly hijacked by your phone. You can keep showing up and still slowly lose yourself.

But the principles of getting your life back have eerie similarities.

The environment is different. The substance is different. The consequences are quieter. But the pattern is familiar: we reach for pleasure, we call it relief, and then we wonder why we don't have the thing we actually crave.

Joy.

Joy is not the same as stimulation. Joy is not the same as a hit. Joy doesn't come from being entertained. Joy is what rises when your life is aligned—when your spirit is connected, when your mind is clear, when your attention is present, when you're living in truth instead of running from it.

And that's why the first letter of the PRECEPT Framework is PRAY.

The First Letter is Going to Bother Some of You

I need to say something clearly before we go any further. The first letter of PRECEPT is going to bother some of you. Others will feel relief, like you've been waiting for someone to finally say it out loud. Either reaction makes sense.

Prayer can be a comfort, and prayer can be a trigger.

If you've been wounded by religion, if you've watched "God talk" used as a weapon, if you've felt shamed under spiritual language, or if you've tried praying before and felt nothing but silence, you may already be bracing yourself.

I'm not asking you to pretend certainty you don't have. I'm not asking you to endorse anyone's version of God as a prerequisite for being helped. What I'm asking for—at the beginning—is something smaller and more honest.

Willingness.

That's the posture "We Agnostics" aims for when it speaks to people who are doubtful and resistant. It doesn't begin by congratulating you for having the right beliefs. It begins by naming the real dilemma: *lack of power* (www.aa.com).

And it's hard to overstate how important that is, because lack of power is what people feel when they're hijacked—whether by alcohol, cocaine, gambling, pornography, work, anger, or the quiet loop of a screen they keep reaching for even when they promised themselves they wouldn't.

"Lack of power, that was our dilemma," the Big Book says. We needed a power by which we could live, and it had to be greater than ourselves (www.aa.com).

That sentence isn't theology. It's diagnosis.

The Thief and the Life We Actually Want

There's a reason the language of Scripture has followed me all these years, especially one verse that frames this entire book's theme.

Jesus said, *"The thief comes only to steal and kill and destroy; I have come that they may have life, and have it to the full."*

The enemy of your inner life is not always a dramatic evil. Often it's a slow theft. A little presence here. A little clarity there. A little patience. A little depth. A little joy.

That's what Part I was about: naming how the modern world fractures attention, hijacks chemistry, and then acts surprised when we feel anxious, thin, reactive, and tired.

But Part II is about the other half of that verse—the life we actually want.

A full life doesn't begin with better time management. It begins with being awake.

Prayer is how you wake up.

PRAY: Connection Before Action

There is a moment in every leader's life when the weight becomes real. Some people feel it the first time they lead a team. Others feel it when a marriage gets strained, when a child starts struggling, when money tightens, when conflict shows up at work, when the pressure mounts and you can feel your nervous system start running the day.

For me, the weight shows up most often when I step into the morning already behind—already stressed—already thinking about five conversations I need to have and ten problems waiting at my doorstep.

For years, I tried to push through that weight with competence. Skill. Experience. Strategy. Grit. And that approach works—until it doesn't. You can win the immediate moment through force, but your internal state is wrong. Your presence is off. You lead from pressure instead of purpose. You speak with urgency instead of wisdom. You react faster than you listen.

Prayer is the alignment step.

Prayer is connection before action.

Without prayer, the rest of PRECEPT can become a self-help routine—useful, even healthy, but still centered on you trying to muscle your way into a better life.

With prayer, PRECEPT becomes something else. It becomes a way of life that changes you from the inside out, because it begins where change always begins: not with your calendar, but with your heart.

Why Jesus Prayed

If there was ever someone who did not "need" prayer, it would have been Jesus. And yet Scripture shows Him praying constantly—early in the morning, late at night, before major decisions, before teaching, before stepping into suffering.

He prayed when people were pulling on Him with needs. He prayed when He was misunderstood. He prayed before choosing His disciples. He prayed before the cross.

Jesus did not pray to perform a ritual. He prayed because leadership requires dependence, not independence. He prayed because He refused to operate disconnected. Prayer was not an accessory to His life; it was the source line.

If Jesus needed prayer, I certainly need it. Every modern leader needs it. Anyone trying to live with purpose needs it.

And when you study His life, a pattern emerges: prayer was His reset, His refuge, His compass, His connection. It was both His quiet place and His preparation place.

We rush past prayer all the time. Jesus didn't.

Watch and Pray: the Warning Most of Us Ignore

One of the most vivid moments in Scripture is the garden. Jesus takes Peter, James, and John with Him on the night of His arrest. He knows what is coming. He knows the emotional and spiritual weight they are about to face. He asks them to stay awake and pray.

He goes a short distance away and begins praying in agony.

When He returns, He finds them sleeping.

And He says to Peter, in essence, *You couldn't stay awake? Watch and pray so you don't fall into temptation.*

That moment isn't mainly about criticizing tired friends. It's a warning about what happens when your inner life is unprepared for pressure. Jesus knew the fight ahead wouldn't be physical first. It would be internal: fear, confusion, despair, temptation, self-protection, the instinct to run.

Prayer strengthens you before the test.

Distraction weakens you before the test.

Most of us learn that the hard way.

What Prayer Actually Does (Bigger Than Most People Think)

Most people have a too-small view of prayer. They think prayer is only asking for things. Sometimes it is. But prayer is more than requests. Prayer is alignment. Prayer is regulation. Prayer is returning.

When you begin the Lord's Prayer with "Our Father," you aren't performing religious language. You're remembering identity. You're reminding your nervous system that you are not alone in the world, not abandoned to pressure, not defined by performance. You are grounded in relationship.

When you say, "Your kingdom come, Your will be done," you're doing something even more countercultural: you're surrendering control. You're choosing trust over anxiety. You're stepping out of the illusion that you can manage the entire world with your own vigilance.

When you pray for "daily bread," you're shrinking your panic down to a size that can be carried. The future is heavy. Today is manageable. Prayer teaches the soul to live in the size of the day.

When you pray, "forgive us as we forgive," something hidden comes into view: resentment is not just a moral issue. It's a leadership issue. You cannot lead well when your inner world is full of static. You cannot listen well when you are carrying irritation. Unresolved conflict drains energy and narrows perspective. Prayer clears the clutter.

A SIMPLE DEFINITION

Prayer is not a performance.
Prayer is alignment.
Prayer is returning to God before
you return to the world.

And when you pray, "lead us not into temptation," notice what you're admitting. You're admitting you are vulnerable. You are admitting you can be pulled off course. You are asking for strength before weakness shows up.

That's the difference between prayer and willpower.

Willpower waits until the moment is here and then tries to fight.

Prayer prepares the soul before the moment arrives.

How to Pray (Start Simple, Then Grow)

In recovery, most people begin with a foxhole prayer because that's where they are. The simple, honest prayer is often the truest starting point:

God, if You're there, please help.

I don't despise that prayer. I respect it. It's honest. It's human. It's the first crack in the wall of self-reliance.

But over time people want more than desperation. They want a way to pray when they're not in crisis. They want a rhythm that can carry them when they're stressed, distracted, reactive, or numb.

This is why the Lord's Prayer is so powerful. It isn't just a script to repeat; it's an anatomy. It's a pattern you can grow into.

Here is that pattern in plain language—not as a religious assignment, but as a daily alignment:

- Start with connection. Remind yourself who God is and who you are.
- Align your heart. Ask for God's will to shape your will.
- Ask for what you need today. Not ten years from now—today.
- Clear the heart. Receive forgiveness and release forgiveness.
- Ask for protection and strength. Not just from "evil," but from the things that devour your attention and distort your peace.

And if that feels like too much, start even smaller. Start with one sentence:

God, please help me get free from the screens and restore my mind, so I can have joy—and that peace that transcends all understanding.

That prayer doesn't require theological sophistication. It requires honesty. And honesty is where transformation begins.

Why Prayer Belongs First in PRECEPT

PRAY is first because it is the foundation that keeps the rest from becoming mere behavior modification.

It is easy to turn self-improvement into another form of striving. It is easy to treat personal growth like a scorecard. It is easy to measure your worth by your consistency, your streak, your output.

Prayer dismantles that.

Prayer begins with relationship, not performance.

Prayer corrects your state before you step into the day. It changes *how* you show up. And leadership—at work, at home, in marriage, in friendship—is always more about how you show up than what you know.

Circumstances don't defeat leaders as often as misalignment defeats them. We walk into the day carrying stress instead of strength, fear instead of faith, insecurity instead of identity. We try to lead from an unstable internal place and then wonder why everything feels heavy.

Prayer reclaims you before the world tries to claim you.

And that's why we start here.

POINTS TO REMEMBER

Prayer is controversial for some people not because they are bad, but because many have been wounded, shamed, pressured, or disappointed by what they were told "God" is supposed to be like. That resistance deserves respect, not argument. The doorway into prayer is not certainty; it's willingness.

The deeper issue underneath distraction is not information—it is regulation. We don't reach for screens only because we want content; we reach because we want relief. Prayer is the first practice in PRECEPT because it restores connection before action. It aligns the heart, steadies the nervous system, clears the relational static, and prepares you for temptation before it arrives.

Finally, prayer does not have to start complicated. The foxhole prayer is a legitimate beginning. "God, if You're there, please help" is not childish—it's honest. And honesty is the start of freedom. In the next chapter, we'll take that honesty and turn it into rhythm, so prayer becomes something you can actually live, even in a distracted world.

(And yes—Chapter 7 will be the practical rhythm: small steps, simple habits, and what to do when prayer feels awkward or empty.)

CHAPTER 7

The Rhythm of Prayer

She was already there when he walked in, seated at the small table near the window where the light fell soft and forgiving across the surface of her coffee. The café had the gentle hush of a Saturday morning—murmured conversations, the occasional scrape of a chair, the steady hiss of the espresso machine behind the counter. It should have felt restful. It should have felt like a pause. But the week had followed her in anyway, clinging to her posture and her face the way fatigue does when it has been earning overtime.

Her coach greeted her without urgency and sat down across from her. He didn't begin with pep talk or strategy. He simply watched her for a moment—how she held her mug as if it were something warm enough to steady her, how her shoulders stayed lifted like she was bracing for impact even though the week was over. He had seen this pattern in a hundred different lives: people who carried so much responsibility that they forgot what it felt like to be unburdened.

When he spoke, his voice was calm, almost conversational, as if they were discussing something practical, like sleep or hydration.

"Let's start where the framework starts," he said. "Pray."

The word landed and she stiffened. It was subtle, but he saw it. A slight tightening around her eyes. A microsecond of recoil before she straightened herself into the posture of someone who has already decided.

"I don't have time to pray," she said.

It wasn't a throwaway line. It was her armor. It was the sentence she had used to protect her life from one more demand. There were only so many things a person could do in a day, and she had spent years building a schedule that felt like a dam holding back a flood. Prayer, to her, belonged to people who had margin—people who weren't managing a household, a career, a thousand small expectations, and a mind that never shut off. Prayer sounded like another task she'd start and fail at. Another thing she'd disappoint herself with.

Her coach didn't challenge the statement directly. He knew that if he argued with her, she would only dig in deeper. Instead, he tilted his head slightly, as if considering her words with respect.

"All right," he said. "Then let's talk about time."

Her expression flickered—part irritation, part exhaustion. Time was the only thing she couldn't talk her way into having. Time was the reason she felt permanently behind even when she was functioning. It was the currency she spent all day without ever seeing what she had bought.

He didn't ask her to trust his opinion. He didn't ask her to introspect. He did what good coaches do when emotions are loud and stories are rehearsed: he reached for reality.

"Do you have your phone?" he asked.

She let out a short breath that wasn't quite a laugh. "Of course."

"Open your screen-time report," he said, not accusing, just steady. "Let's make this concrete."

She hesitated, but she also felt a strange relief. Data would prove her point. Data would shut this down. She wasn't reckless with her phone. She wasn't the kind of person who scrolled for hours. She used it for work. For coordination. For staying connected. For little moments of mental relief in between everything else. Normal life.

She unlocked the phone and navigated to the report quickly, almost eagerly. When the number appeared, she turned the screen toward him with a quiet confidence that felt, for a moment, like vindication.

"See?" she said. "It's not that much."

He glanced at it and nodded, as if he were acknowledging her effort. His expression didn't change, which unsettled her slightly. She had expected surprise, maybe an apology, maybe a concession.

Then he asked, gently, "Can I see it?"

The request was so normal, so unthreatening, that she didn't even think. She slid the phone across the table.

He took it the way a surgeon takes an instrument: carefully, without drama. His thumb moved once across the screen.

Back one day.

Friday.

He held the phone for a moment without speaking. The café noise continued around them, ordinary and oblivious. But at their table, the air changed.

Friday's report was not a simple number. It was a list. It was a trail.

Instagram. Snapchat. Facebook. LinkedIn. TikTok. Amazon. Pinterest. X.

Two more apps sat beneath them—icons he didn't recognize, names that meant nothing to him but obviously meant something to her, because she went still when she saw them there. It wasn't the variety that was most painful. It was the sheer accumulation of minutes, stacked in tidy little rows, each one representing a moment she hadn't felt slipping away.

Her face warmed as if the truth had heat. She stared at the screen and tried, instinctively, to explain it before she could even find the words. Friday had been a hard week. Not the kind of hard that comes with a single dramatic event, but the exhausting, grinding kind—the kind that drains you by inches. She had come home with her mind buzzing and her body tired, wanting something that would take the edge off without asking anything of her. She remembered the clink of ice in a glass, the first sip of wine, the quiet permission she gave herself because she deserved relief. Then another glass, because the first didn't quite quiet her thoughts. And then the familiar drift toward the couch, toward the glow, toward the scroll that promised rest and delivered nothing but a strange, foggy emptiness.

She hadn't called it a binge then. She had dressed it up in nicer words: unwinding, decompressing, staying connected, distracting herself from the pressure. But looking at it now—seeing it itemized like a receipt—she felt the embarrassment deepen into something more honest.

Grief.

Not grief like tragedy. Grief like a quiet loss you can't unsee once you name it. Those weren't just minutes. Those were the few scraps of her evening, the narrow window where she could have recovered, connected, reflected, or simply been present. And she had spent them the way a person spends loose change—without noticing until it's gone.

Her coach finally turned the phone back toward her and spoke softly, not as a rebuke, but as an observation.

"I think you might be able to find time."

He didn't say it sharply. He didn't press it. He didn't pile on. He let the statement stand, because it was sturdy enough to hold its own.

She lowered her eyes and nodded, once, almost imperceptibly. The defensiveness she brought into the café didn't vanish, but it lost its charge. It was hard to argue with a mirror that didn't hate you.

"So what," she said after a moment, the words quieter now, less rehearsed. "Five minutes?"

He shook his head slightly. "Start with two."

She looked up, skeptical again at the simplicity, as if in her world anything that small couldn't possibly matter. "Two minutes won't change my life."

"No," he agreed. "But it can change your state. And your state changes what you reach for next."

She sat with that. She knew what he meant even if she didn't want to admit it. The phone didn't take over her life in one dramatic decision. It took over in moments—tiny, invisible moments when she felt stressed, tired, lonely, restless, or simply empty. If she could interrupt the first moment, maybe she could change what happened after it.

"What do I even say?" she asked.

Her coach's voice stayed steady. "Say the truth," he replied. "That's where prayer starts."

She stared at the table as if the wood grain might offer her a script. She didn't want to perform. She didn't want to pretend she was full of faith when she wasn't even sure what she believed some days. But she could tell the truth. She could do that much.

Her lips parted, and the sentence came out like something fragile she was placing in open hands.

"God... help me."

No surge. No mystical warmth. No cinematic transformation. Just the beginning of a rhythm—small enough to be repeatable, honest enough to be real. And for the first time in a long time, she felt a thin edge of relief that wasn't borrowed from a screen.

Not because her life had changed in the café.

Because she had.

■　■　■　■

The moment at that table was not primarily about technology. The screen-time report simply did what numbers often do: it made a hidden pattern undeniable. What changed her wasn't a statistic; it was the sudden clarity that "I don't have time" was not a time problem at all. It was an attention problem. Her life wasn't lacking minutes; it was leaking them, quietly, in the places she didn't track and didn't name, and the leaking had become so normal that she couldn't feel it until she saw it.

Prayer matters because it interrupts that drift at the exact point it begins. Most people think their problem is the phone, but the phone is only the instrument. The deeper problem is the reflex. When discomfort rises—stress, loneliness, boredom, fatigue—your body reaches for relief before your mind even debates it. The screen is fast relief. It is instant, effortless, and familiar, and that is why it becomes the default. Prayer is not first in the PRECEPT Framework because it is the most "religious" discipline. It is first because it is the first substitution. It is the first deliberate choice to reach for connection instead of escape.

This is where many readers get stuck. They assume prayer requires a certain mood, vocabulary, or uninterrupted block of time, so they postpone it until life calms down. But life rarely calms down. It becomes full. That is why prayer—if it is going to be real—has to fit the life you actually have, not the life you wish you had. The goal is not to become someone who prays beautifully. The goal is to become someone who returns consistently.

If you want a starting point that works for busy people, skeptical people, exhausted people, and distracted people, start here: pray for two minutes before you touch your phone in the morning. Not after you check messages. Not after you scan headlines. Not after you "just see what came in." The first voice of your day shapes your state. If your day begins with the world's noise, you will carry that noise forward, and much of your day will be reactive. If your day begins with connection, you have a chance to move through it with steadiness and intention. Two minutes will not reorganize your schedule, but it can begin to reorganize you.

Two minutes often feels too small to matter, especially for people who are already overwhelmed. That is exactly why it works. You are not trying to win a contest of spiritual discipline. You are training a reflex. You are replacing the first reach—the reach for stimulation and relief—with a return that restores instead of drains. If two minutes feels like too much, begin with one minute. If one minute feels like too much, begin with thirty seconds. Your goal is not length. Your goal is repetition. The thief steals in small moments, which means freedom is reclaimed in small moments too.

The question that comes next is always the same: what do I say? Many people avoid prayer because they imagine it must sound holy or certain. But prayer is not a speech, and it is not a performance. Prayer is a relationship, and relationships begin the same way every time: with honesty. If you don't know what to say, say what is true. If you aren't sure God is there, say that. If you are angry, say that. If you are ashamed, say that. If you are exhausted and scattered and you keep reaching for your phone as a way to numb the pressure, say that too. The most faithful prayer is not the most polished prayer. The most faithful prayer is the one you actually pray.

For many people, the best starting prayer is a single sentence: "God, help me." It doesn't sound sophisticated, but it is honest. It doesn't require you to pretend. It simply pulls you back to the truth that you are not meant to manage life alone. If you want a slightly longer version that remains direct, you might pray, "God, restore my mind and make me present today," or, "God, lead me before I get pulled." A sentence like that, prayed consistently, does more than most people realize because it gradually builds awareness. You begin to notice the moment you are about to drift, and you discover that you have a choice. That awareness is not small. Awareness is the beginning of freedom.

This is also where the second "P" comes into view: practice. Prayer is not merely a belief; it is a practice that forms you through repetition. You can understand prayer intellectually and still never do it, in the same way you can understand exercise and still never move your body. What changes a person is not one emotional moment but a rhythm. The nervous system learns through pattern. The mind learns through repetition. If screens have become your reflexive comfort object—the thing you reach for when you are bored, lonely, stressed, or depleted—then prayer becomes your new reflex, not as a rule, but as a replacement. You are training yourself to reach for connection instead of escape.

Sometimes, early on, a simple structure can help, not because prayer is a formula, but because distracted minds benefit from rails. This is where the PRAY framework is useful. Begin with praise, not because God needs compliments, but because you need perspective. Praise lifts your eyes above your stress and reminds you that your circumstances are not the full story. Then repent, not as self-hatred, but as clearing the static. Repentance is simply naming drift and asking to return. Next, ask. Bring your real needs without pretending you are fine. Ask for clarity, steadiness, courage, patience, joy, and freedom from the patterns that are stealing your attention. Finally, yield. Yield is the quiet "yes" at the end, the decision to trust that God's will is wiser than your impulses, and that surrender is not a loss but the beginning of peace. The purpose of a framework like this is not to make prayer mechanical; it is to make prayer accessible when your mind is too loud to know where to begin.

A prayer rhythm that only works on calm days will not survive Monday. That is why I recommend anchoring prayer to moments that already exist in your life, rather than waiting for perfect conditions. The first anchor is your two minutes before the phone in the morning, which becomes the daily act of alignment. The second anchor is a brief return prayer in the middle of the day—ten seconds when you feel yourself getting hijacked, a short sentence that brings you back. The third anchor is a doorway prayer before important moments, the kind of prayer you whisper before a meeting, a hard conversation, or a decision. The fourth anchor is an evening review that helps you end the day with reflection instead of fog, noticing where you were aligned, where you drifted, what you need to release, and what you want to practice tomorrow. Over time these anchors begin to reshape your attention, because they create repeated moments when you practice presence instead of escape.

If you take anything from this chapter, let it be this: prayer will not feel powerful at first because you are not using it to perform holiness. You are using it to retrain a habit of mind. Two minutes feels small until you remember what you are replacing. If you can spend hours in the glow of a screen—not because you are weak but because you are human—then you can reclaim two minutes, not as a rule but as a lifeline. The thief steals in minutes. Freedom returns the same way.

THE FIRST REACH

Most people think their problem is the phone. It usually isn't. The phone is just the fastest answer to a deeper question: How do I get relief right now? The moment you feel stress, boredom, loneliness, fatigue, or frustration, your

*body reaches before your mind decides. That first reach is
the hinge point. If you reach for a screen, you train your
nervous system to associate discomfort with escape. If you
reach for prayer, you train your nervous system to associate
discomfort with connection. Freedom often begins one
decision earlier than you think: not when you stop scrolling,
but when you interrupt the reflex that starts the scroll.*

A TWO-MINUTE PRAYER YOU CAN ACTUALLY PRAY

*If you don't know what to say, don't perform. Tell the truth.
"God, I'm here. I'm tired. My mind is scattered.
Help me be present today. Restore my mind.
Lead me before I get pulled. I trust You. Amen."*

PRAY (A SIMPLE STRUCTURE WHEN YOU NEED WORDS)

*P—Praise: "God, You are good, and You are here."
R—Repent: "Forgive my drift—my distraction
and my impatience."
A—Ask: "Give me clarity, peace, and strength today."
Y—Yield: "Your will is best. Lead me."
This isn't a formula. It's scaffolding.
Use it until prayer becomes natural.*

POINTS TO REMEMBER

Prayer is the first step in the PRECEPT Framework because it is the first substitution. It is the first intentional choice to reach for connection instead of reaching for escape. In a world that trains you to numb discomfort with quick stimulation, prayer does something quietly radical: it brings you back to yourself and back to God before the day begins spending you.

If you want a starting point that works in real life, keep it simple and specific. Pray for two minutes before you touch your phone in the morning. The point is not to prove anything or to become instantly disciplined; the point is to change what has the first voice in your mind. When the world speaks first, you tend to live reactively. When you begin with prayer, you give your mind and body a chance to start from steadiness rather than urgency.

When you don't know what to say, say what is true. Prayer is not a speech, and it is not a performance. It is a relationship, and relationships begin with honesty. A single sentence—"God, help me"—is not small when it is real. Over time, honest prayers practiced consistently reshape your inner life more than polished words ever will.

Finally, remember that prayer becomes transformative through practice. You are not trying to win a moment; you are building a rhythm. The nervous system is trained through repetition, which means your freedom will grow the same way your distraction grew: one day at a time, one choice at a time, one return at a time.

CHAPTER 8

READ: Feeding Your Mind Something Real

The truck smelled faintly of pine and coffee—fresh air and an old habit. The coach drove with one hand on the wheel, steady and unhurried, the way he did everything. They were headed out of the city toward water, toward quiet, toward the kind of day that felt almost irresponsible to an executive who measured his worth in output. Fishing rods were packed in the back, waders folded neatly beside a small cooler, and on the dashboard the phone sat face down like a compromise.

The executive kept glancing at it anyway.

Not because he had an emergency. Because his body had been trained to check. The reflex was older than any email thread: *Look. Refresh. Make sure you're not missing something. Stay ahead.* It was the same instinct that kept him working late, taking calls on vacations, and proving—over and over again—that he was indispensable. He lived inside a constant low-grade urgency, the kind that doesn't feel like anxiety until you finally step out of it.

The coach didn't mention the phone. He knew better than to start with the symptom. Instead he gave the man space to talk, and the executive filled it the way high performers always do. He talked about deadlines. He talked about a team member who wasn't pulling their weight. He talked about a project that had expanded faster than the budget. He talked about his calendar like it was a weather report—inevitable and somehow personal at the same time.

After a few miles, the coach asked casually, "What are you feeding your mind right now?"

The executive blinked. "What do you mean?"

"Books," the coach said. "What are you reading?"

That's when the resistance appeared—not anger, not defiance, just the tired certainty of someone who had already made up his mind. "I don't have time to read," he said, as if the sentence should end the conversation.

The coach nodded, letting it land. He didn't shame him. He didn't argue. He kept his eyes on the road and asked, "Is that true, or is that a conclusion?"

The executive let out a short, humorless laugh. "It's true. I'm in meetings all day. I'm up early. I'm exhausted at night. I can barely keep up with what's coming at me, let alone sit down with a book."

The coach's voice stayed calm. "I believe you're busy. I'm not disputing that. I'm asking something else. When you do have quiet moments—waiting rooms, lines, the minutes before a meeting starts—where does your mind go?"

The executive didn't answer immediately. He knew the answer. They both did. His mind went to the quickest available relief. It went to the feed. It went to the scroll. It went to the endless stream of content that felt like information but rarely became wisdom.

The coach continued, not as a lecture but as a diagnosis spoken with compassion. "Most people don't stop reading because they hate books," he said. "They stop reading because screens trained them to live on speed. Reading requires surrendering to the pace of something deeper. It forces your attention to stay in one place long enough to be formed. That can feel foreign when your mind has been fractured for years."

The executive looked out the window at the passing trees, the highway unwinding like a ribbon toward somewhere quieter. He didn't want to admit it, but he felt exposed—not because the coach had accused him, but because the question had revealed a truth he already suspected. The reason he didn't read wasn't merely time. It was that his attention had been conditioned. He lived in a world of constant inputs, and it had made him quick, reactive, and productive—while slowly thinning out something else inside him.

The coach didn't press him for a confession. He just said, "Let's not make this complicated today. Let's treat reading the way we treat nutrition. If you feed your body nothing but sugar, you will feel wired and exhausted and hungry all at once. If you feed your mind nothing but noise, the same thing happens. You become stimulated, but not strengthened."

That line stayed in the cab like a quiet challenge. The executive didn't respond, but his face softened slightly. Not agreement. Something closer to recognition.

The coach turned off the highway onto a smaller road, and the landscape opened up. Fewer billboards. Fewer lights. More sky. The world felt less like a machine and more like a place where humans were meant to live. As they drove, the coach said something that sounded simple but carried weight: "You don't need more information. You need formation."

That's what reading is. Reading is not entertainment. Reading is not a hobby reserved for people with extra time. Reading is one of the most practical ways to feed your mind something real in an age designed to keep you mentally malnourished. Screens stimulate. Books strengthen. Screens specialize in reaction. Books build reflection. Screens feed you fragments. Books form you into a person who can hold an idea long enough for it to reshape you.

If the first discipline—prayer—aligns the heart, reading begins to reform the mind. Together they do something powerful: they pull you out of reactivity and return you to intention. That is why reading belongs at the front of the PRECEPT Framework. Not because everyone should become an academic, but because a scattered mind cannot sustain a meaningful life. You cannot lead well with a mind that has been trained to skip, scroll, and react. And you cannot repair a fractured attention span by consuming more fragments of content. You repair it by practicing depth.

What is happening to us is not subtle anymore. The modern world is desperate for your attention, and it has gotten good at taking it. Most of us live under a steady drizzle of inputs: headlines, notifications, clips, hot takes, and endless "updates." It all feels important in the moment, but it rarely becomes wisdom. In fact, much of it does the opposite. It keeps your mind in a constant state of partial focus—busy, stimulated, and strangely unfulfilled. You can spend hours consuming and still feel empty, because consumption is not the same thing as nourishment.

Reading is nourishment. It slows your mind down long enough for substance to become strength. It rebuilds patience. It rebuilds attention. It rebuilds imagination. It gives you words for what you feel but can't articulate. It gives you frameworks for problems you thought were unique to you. It introduces you to people who have endured, failed, rebuilt, and learned. It trains you to think in paragraphs instead of fragments, to reason instead of react, to interpret instead of mimic. The older I get, the more convinced I am that many of the problems people call "stress" are actually symptoms of shallow inputs. When your mind is fed on noise, your inner life becomes noisy. When your mind is fed on truth, your inner life becomes steadier.

That steadiness becomes a leadership advantage whether you intend it or not. When you read widely and deeply, you develop something that cannot be faked: perspective. You begin to recognize patterns in people and organizations. You become less surprised by human nature. You learn how fear hides behind anger, how insecurity hides behind control, how shame turns into blame, and how boredom turns into addiction. You also become more patient with others because you see more clearly how people become who they are. Reading gives you empathy without sentimentality. It gives you compassion without naivety. It forms you into the kind of leader whose presence calms a room rather than electrifies it with tension.

I've learned this as a coach and consultant: there is no substitute for being well-read. Not because reading makes you smarter in a showy way, but because it gives you a library of wisdom you can draw from when life gets complicated. When someone comes to you with a marriage that feels brittle, or a team that's drifting, or an addiction that's resurfacing, or a career that feels hollow, you don't need a motivational quote. You need a deeper grasp of what people are, what they're prone to, and what helps them become whole again. Reading gives you that. It gives you metaphors and examples, cautionary tales and redemptive ones. It gives you language. It gives you frameworks. It gives you a steadier mind, which means you don't lead from whatever emotion happens to be loudest that day.

But reading is not only practical. It is also spiritual formation for anyone who is open to that reality. If you read Scripture regularly, you begin to recognize what wisdom sounds like. You begin to hear the difference between depth and hype, between truth and sophistication, between conviction and emotional manipulation. The Bible is not simply information to store; it is revelation that shapes how you see God, how you see yourself, and how you see reality. Over time, it forms your morality, your worldview, your patience, your compassion, your resilience, and your discernment. It trains you to recognize counterfeits because you've been living with the real thing long enough to hear the difference.

In a way, every good book also becomes a kind of friendship. A quiet mentor. A conversation with someone whose life you could never fully live, whose experiences you might never have, but whose wisdom can still reach you. Reading is one of the only practices that allows wisdom to travel across time. It puts you in the room with leaders, thinkers, saints, scientists, historians, psychologists, and storytellers. Some books walk beside you for a week. Others follow you for the rest of your life. Your world expands, not because you "know more," but because you become more capable of understanding complexity without panic.

That expansion, however, requires discernment. The more you read, the more you realize not every celebrated book deserves your attention. Some books have hype but not wisdom. Some have cleverness but not character. Some are persuasive in the way fast content is persuasive—because they flatter ego, promise shortcuts, and sell certainty. I've had the experience of reading a book everyone swore by and feeling, deep down, that something was off. Sometimes you can't explain it in the moment; you just sense the difference between truth and performance. Over time, the more you read—and the more you live—the more that discernment sharpens. You begin to value authors who have actually done something, endured something, sacrificed something, built something real, failed and learned, and come out wiser. You start to recognize that wisdom tends to carry humility, and truth usually sounds steadier than hype.

This is one reason I encourage reading widely. If your worldview is grounded, it won't be threatened by understanding. Wisdom is not fragile. Real faith is not brittle. You can read outside your bubble and remain anchored; in fact, it often strengthens your anchor because it forces you to think, to compare, to examine, and to discern rather than simply absorb. The goal isn't to become cynical or endlessly skeptical. The goal is to become discerning—able to recognize truth, able to recognize counterfeit, able to recognize what nourishes your soul and what merely stimulates your chemistry.

If prayer is connection before action, reading becomes wisdom before action. Prayer re-centers your heart. Reading re-forms your mind. Together they build an internal life strong enough to withstand an environment designed to fracture you. That's why these practices feel different than most "self-help." Self-help is often about acquiring techniques. PRECEPT is about becoming a different kind of person. Formation always happens through inputs. You are shaped by what you consume, what you meditate on, what you internalize. Your life will rise or fall to the level of your inputs.

The executive in the passenger seat didn't need a book list in that moment. He needed a reframe. He needed permission to stop treating reading like a luxury and start treating it like fuel. He needed to see that the "I don't have time" story was not a final truth. It was a reflection of where his attention had been trained to go when he was tired. The coach wasn't trying to add another demand to his week. He was trying to give him a substitute that would strengthen him instead of drain him.

SCREENS STIMULATE, BOOKS STRENGTHEN

A screen can flood your brain with stimulation and still leave you mentally underfed. A good book does the opposite: it may feel slower in the moment, but it strengthens your ability to focus, think, discern, and lead. If you want wisdom, you don't binge it. You grow into it.

The truck rolled closer to the river, and the road narrowed, and the world quieted the way it does when you step away from the machinery. The coach didn't say much after that. He didn't need to. The point wasn't for the executive to feel guilty; guilt rarely transforms anyone. The point was to plant a different idea: that he could feed his mind something real again. He could become the kind of person whose attention lasted longer than a headline, whose inner life had depth enough to hold pressure without breaking, and whose leadership came from reflection rather than reaction.

Reading is one of the simplest and most countercultural ways to reclaim your mind. It builds you slowly. It strengthens you steadily. It reunites your attention, which is exactly what the distraction economy has been trying to fracture. And once your mind begins to heal, you can start to build a reading habit that actually sticks—one that fits a busy life, one that begins small, and one that becomes part of who you are. That is what the next chapter is for.

A screen can flood your brain with stimulation and still leave you mentally underfed. A good book does the opposite: it may feel slower in the moment, but it strengthens your ability to focus, think, discern, and lead. If you want wisdom, you don't binge it. You grow into it.

POINTS TO REMEMBER

Reading is not entertainment or an elite hobby; it is formation. It feeds your mind something real in a world that profits from keeping your attention fragmented. When your inputs are shallow, your inner life becomes noisy and reactive. When your inputs are wise, your inner life becomes steadier and more resilient.

Prayer aligns the heart, but reading forms the mind. If prayer is connection before action, reading is wisdom before action. Leaders who read tend to lead from reflection rather than reaction, because reading builds perspective, language, empathy, and discernment over time.

Finally, the common objection—"I don't have time to read"—is often less about the calendar and more about conditioned attention. The deeper question is not whether you have time, but what you reach for when you're tired. Reading becomes a substitute that restores rather than drains, and it opens the door to a habit that can be built realistically and sustainably.

As the coach eased the truck into the gravel pull-off and killed the engine, the executive sat for a moment longer than he needed to, as if his mind were still catching up to the quieter world outside the windshield. He didn't feel inspired in a dramatic way. What he felt was more practical—and, in its own way, more hopeful: the sense that this didn't have to be an all-or-nothing overhaul. If his attention had been trained in small moments of escape, it could be rebuilt in small moments of return. The next step, then, wasn't finding the perfect book or carving out heroic blocks of time; it was learning how to start so small it would be almost impossible to fail, and repeating that start until it became part of who he was.

CHAPTER 9

How to Build a Reading Habit
That Actually Sticks

I remember the first book I ever read. I was in first grade—six years old—and I carried that little book home like it was proof I could do something important. I sat down in the living room and read it out loud to my mom and dad, feeling their attention fall on me like sunlight. I can still picture their faces. I can still feel the pride rising in my chest as the words came out right. I had wanted to read for as long as I could remember, and now I could.

What I didn't know then was that the story would take a turn.

By third grade my teachers started noticing patterns I couldn't explain. Letters flipped. Words blended. Lines seemed to move. Reading took far more energy than it should have, and the harder I tried to force it the more exhausted I became. That's when dyslexia entered my life. I didn't fully understand what it meant until much later, but I understood its effect immediately: reading would never come easy. While other kids tore through books, I fought to keep up. While others could read a chapter in twenty minutes, it took me an hour. While others enjoyed reading, I endured it.

That struggle shaped how I saw myself. It shaped my confidence. It shaped my habits. It became one more place where I could quietly decide I wasn't "that kind of person"—not the kind who read, not the kind who loved books, not the kind who could sit still long enough to absorb something deep. And when you make that decision early, it follows you. It becomes a story you tell yourself. Stories do that. They don't just describe your life—they build it.

Even so, another story was forming underneath that one.

At sixteen, not long after my parents separated, my dad gathered my brothers and me together and opened a book: *How to Win Friends and Influence People.* He didn't hand it to us and tell us to "go read." He read it to us out loud, page by page, chapter by chapter. Something about that mattered. It wasn't only the content. It was the posture. My dad wasn't trying to raise bookworms. He was trying to raise men who could navigate life with wisdom. And for reasons I couldn't have explained at the time, that book planted a seed: reading could change you.

When he stopped reading, I kept going.

I didn't suddenly become an effortless reader. Dyslexia didn't evaporate. But the category changed. Reading wasn't just schoolwork anymore. It wasn't just something you did because a teacher required it. Reading became something you did because you wanted to grow. That shift—the shift from obligation to formation—is the beginning of a reading habit that sticks.

Years later, in my early twenties, I started spending time with wise business owners—men who had built real companies, men who had endured hard seasons, men who had the kind of calm you can't fake. Almost every one of them said the same thing to me, in almost the same words: "Read two pages a day."

Two pages. Not a chapter. Not an hour. Not a book a week. Two pages.

At first that sounded almost ridiculous. Two pages felt like nothing. But I learned quickly that two pages is not about quantity. Two pages is about identity. Two pages is about showing up. It's about proving to yourself—quietly, consistently—that you are the kind of person who reads. And when you show up long enough, even in small ways, something shifts. A habit stops being a decision you fight for and becomes a rhythm you return to.

Those two pages weren't easy for me. Dyslexia made reading slow. Insecurity made it intimidating. Some days I read one page. Some days I read a paragraph. Some days I reread the same page twice because I couldn't retain the thread. But I stayed with it. I showed up, even when it was clumsy. Two pages became four. Four became ten. Ten became the habit of a lifetime. Today I get through more books in a year than most people get through in a decade—not because I'm gifted, but because I built a habit one slow page at a time.

This chapter isn't really about reading. It's about becoming the kind of person who can read consistently in a world designed to make that difficult.

The modern environment is not friendly to deep attention. It trains you to skim. It trains you to scroll. It trains you to chase novelty. Then you sit down with a book and wonder why your mind wanders after three paragraphs. Nothing is wrong with you. Your attention has been conditioned. The same system that trained you to consume fragments can retrain you to absorb substance, but it requires a different approach than most people take. The mistake most people make is trying to build a reading habit with intensity. They attempt an ambitious plan—an hour a day, a book a week, a stack of titles waiting on the nightstand—and then life happens, they miss a day, and the entire plan collapses under shame. That's not how habits are built. Habits are not built through intensity. They're built through consistency.

That's the sobriety lesson too. People think recovery happens through a single dramatic moment of willpower. It rarely does. It happens the way real change always happens: one day at a time, one decision at a time. A day becomes a week. A week becomes a month. A month becomes a year. Years become a life. The same principle applies to attention. The same principle applies to reading. Not intensity—consistency. Not pressure—practice. Not fear—identity.

If you struggle to read consistently, it's usually for one of three reasons.

First, you believe reading requires long blocks of time. You imagine a perfect scenario: a quiet house, an hour of uninterrupted margin, a comfortable chair, a cup of coffee, the right mood. And because real life rarely offers that scenario, you never start. But reading doesn't require an hour. Reading requires a beginning. Five minutes is enough. Ten minutes is plenty. A few pages is a win. If you wait until you have a full hour, you'll wait the rest of your life.

Second, you believe reading has to be smooth and focused to "count." You think if your mind wanders, you failed. If you reread a paragraph, you failed. If you don't remember everything, you failed. That's not reading—that's perfectionism disguised as productivity. Real reading is often slow. Real reading includes rereading. Real reading includes wandering thoughts and returning again. Your attention isn't broken; it's being strengthened. You don't shame a person for shaking during their first workout. You don't shame yourself for wandering during your first return to depth.

Third, you treat reading like a task instead of a transformation. You try to "get through books" the way you get through an inbox, and because it feels like one more chore, you avoid it. The shift that makes reading stick is when you stop asking, "How many pages did I read?" and start asking, "Who am I becoming because I read?" Reading is not a box to check. Reading is formation. When you see it that way, reading becomes something you want—not because it is easy, but because it is nourishing.

So how do you build a reading habit that actually sticks?

You begin embarrassingly small.

That's not a gimmick. It's wisdom. Two pages. One page. One paragraph. One idea. The size doesn't matter in the beginning; the repetition does. Your goal is not endurance. Your goal is identity. You are becoming the kind of person who reads, and identity is built through reality—through doing, not wishing.

Then you pair listening with reading if that helps. Some people feel ashamed to admit they "listen" more than they read, as if audiobooks don't count. That's nonsense. Listening is reading for modern life. Listening builds familiarity. It shapes you while you drive, while you walk, while you do the dishes, while you lift weights. And for people with dyslexia—or for people whose attention has been shredded by screens—listening can be the bridge back into books. Often I listen first, then I read. Hearing it lays down the track; reading it deepens it. Together that combination has changed my life.

Next, you stack reading onto a routine that already exists. Don't invent a new ritual you have to remember. Attach reading to something you already do: coffee, lunch, bedtime, the first ten minutes after prayer, the last ten minutes before sleep. Habit stacking removes the need for constant decision-making. You're not relying on motivation. You're building a groove in your day. And grooves, once worn in, are surprisingly faithful.

You also choose books that strengthen you, not books that impress other people. Ignore hype. Ignore trends. Ignore books people pretend to love but never finish. Read what helps you become wiser, calmer, stronger, kinder, clearer, more grounded, more human. If a book isn't feeding you, put it down without guilt. Reading is too valuable to waste on content that leaves you empty.

As your habit grows, keep a simple list of books you return to. Every leader needs a handful of books they revisit, because some books don't just teach you once—they mentor you in seasons. A good book gives you insight the first time. A great book gives you insight every time. You read the same pages as a different person ten years later, and suddenly you notice what you missed because you weren't ready for it then. Rereading is not repetition; it's revelation. It shows you how you've grown and where you've drifted.

Finally, remember that reading widely strengthens discernment. If you only read what flatters your worldview, you will become confident but shallow. If you read across ideas—history, psychology, theology, biography, spiritual formation—you begin to recognize truth more clearly. Wisdom is not threatened by understanding. It is strengthened by it. You don't read widely to become confused; you read widely to become grounded. You learn the difference between hype and substance, between cleverness and character, between persuasion and truth.

And there is one more element people underestimate: reading changes your state. It slows your breathing. It steadies your mind. It quiets the frantic mental jumping that screens normalize. It rebuilds your ability to focus. In the same way exercise strengthens the body over time, reading strengthens the mind over time. It is training. It is non-dramatic. It is profoundly effective.

The real reward of a reading habit is not the number of books you finish. The reward is the person you become. You become wiser. Calmer. More discerning. More patient. More resilient. You become

TWO PAGES A DAY

Two pages isn't about volume. It's about identity. It's about proving to yourself, quietly and consistently, that you are the kind of person who reads. Endurance comes later. Show up first.

a better leader, spouse, parent, friend. You develop a deeper inner life so you can live a deeper outer life. You gain language for what matters and perspective for what doesn't. You begin to recognize traps faster. You begin to see yourself more clearly. You begin to hear wisdom with a sharper ear.

Reading gives you what screens never will. Screens are fast, but they are thin. Reading is slow, but it is strong. It rebuilds what the distraction economy fractures. It forms you into a person who can hold attention, hold meaning, hold truth. And that kind of person is rare now—which is exactly why the world needs more of them.

Most of all, reading is possible for anyone. Even for the person who thinks they are "not a reader." Even for the person whose attention has been hijacked. Even for the dyslexic kid who struggled through every page. Even for the leader who says they don't have time. Start small. Start again. Two pages. One paragraph. One moment of return. The habit doesn't begin when you finish a book. It begins when you become the kind of person who shows up.

POINTS TO REMEMBER

A reading habit that sticks is built through consistency, not intensity. Start embarrassingly small—two pages, one page, even one paragraph—and repeat it until it becomes normal. The goal early on isn't to finish books; it's to become a reader.

If you struggle, it's usually because you're waiting for long blocks of time, demanding perfect focus, or treating reading like a task instead of formation. Reading strengthens attention the way exercise strengthens the body: through practice, not perfection.

Use support systems that make reading sustainable. Pair audiobooks with reading, stack reading onto an existing routine, choose books that nourish rather than impress, and keep a short list of books worth revisiting. The reward isn't a number of titles—it's the depth and clarity you become.

Recommended Reading List (Expanded)

These books shaped different seasons of my life. Some came during confusion, some during growth, some during failure, and some during rebuilding. Many of them found me at the exact moment I needed wisdom from someone who had simply walked further down the road than I had. This is not a "perfect" list, and it is certainly not the only list. It is a set of markers—books that, in my experience, tend to form leaders, strengthen character, deepen faith, sharpen relationships, and restore a mind that has been thinned out by noise.

Consider this more like a well-worn trail map than a syllabus. You don't need to read everything. You don't need to agree with everything. You don't even need to start with the "best" book. You just need to begin with one book that feeds your mind something real.

PERSONAL GROWTH AND CHARACTER FORMATION

- **Atomic Habits — James Clear:** A practical guide to building small, consistent habits that shape identity and transformation.
- **How to Win Friends and Influence People — Dale Carnegie:** My first life-changing book. Timeless, foundational, and still one of the best relationship guides ever written.
- **Man's Search for Meaning — Viktor Frankl:** A deep, powerful look at suffering, purpose, and the human spirit.
- **Surely You're Joking, Mr. Feynman — Richard Feynman:** A joyful exploration of curiosity and unconventional thinking.
- **You Happier — Daniel Amen:** A practical, brain-based guide to emotional health.
- **The Inner Game of Tennis — W. Timothy Gallwey:** Arguably the best book ever written on mindset, performance, and defeating the mental interference that sabotages growth.

- **AA Big Book:** Whether you are an alcoholic or not, this is one of the most honest books ever written about ego, surrender, community, and spiritual transformation.
- **Coaching for Performance — John Whitmore:** A masterclass on coaching others, developing potential, and leading with presence.
- **Body for Life — Bill Phillips:** A simple, disciplined approach to physical transformation and personal accountability.
- **The Glucose Revolution — Jessie Inchauspé:** A science-based guide to stabilizing energy, improving performance, and understanding metabolic health.

LEADERSHIP AND ORGANIZATIONAL HEALTH

- **Scrum — Jeff Sutherland:** A modern blueprint for building high-performing, aligned, adaptive teams.
- **The 100X Leader — Steve Cockram and Jeremie Kubicek:** A foundational leadership framework that aligns with my coaching and mentoring philosophy.
- **The Advantage — Patrick Lencioni:** The clearest book on organizational health and one of the most important leadership books ever written.
- **The Road Less Stupid — Keith J. Cunningham:** Sharp, blunt wisdom for leaders who want to avoid preventable mistakes and learn to think clearly.
- **The Goal — Eliyahu Goldratt:** A gripping business novel that builds your systems thinking and operational intuition.
- **Getting Things Done — David Allen:** A practical, lifelong system for managing commitments and eliminating mental clutter.
- **Skunk Works — Ben Rich:** A behind-the-scenes look at how elite teams innovate, trust each other, and solve impossible problems.
- **Maximum Volume — Barry Goldsmith:** Powerful insights into creative excellence, collaboration, and the pursuit of mastery.

SALES AND INFLUENCE

- **Let's Get Real or Let's Not Play — Mahan Khalsa:** A values-driven, trust-based approach to selling. Transformational for anyone in sales or consulting.
- **SPIN Selling — Neil Rackham:** A research-backed model for complex, consultative sales. Essential for enterprise work.
- **The Challenger Sale — Matthew Dixon and Brent Adamson:** A book that explains why the most successful sellers teach, tailor, and take control.
- **Sales Management. Simplified. — Mike Weinberg:** A straightforward, no-nonsense blueprint for leading effective sales teams.
- **The Sales Acceleration Formula — Mark Roberge:** A data-driven, scalable approach to sales hiring, training, and growth.
- **The Sales Development Playbook — Trish Bertuzzi:** One of the best resources for building effective SDR teams and systems.

SPIRITUAL GROWTH AND THEOLOGY

- **The Bible:** Nothing shapes character and wisdom like Scripture. I read it every year.
- **The Reason for God — Timothy Keller:** A thoughtful, deeply grounded explanation of Christian faith in the modern world.
- **I Don't Have Enough Faith to Be an Atheist — Geisler and Turek:** A logical, evidence-based exploration of faith and truth.
- **Knowing Scripture — R. C. Sproul:** A trusted guide on how to read, interpret, and understand Scripture with depth.
- **Love Does — Bob Goff:** A joyful vision of faith expressed through action and kindness.

HEALTH, LONGEVITY, AND HUMAN PERFORMANCE

- **Outlive — Peter Attia:** One of the most important books on long-term health and vitality.
- **History and Biography: The Wright Brothers — David McCullough:** A powerful portrait of grit, risk, craftsmanship, and belief.

- **Steve Jobs — Walter Isaacson:** An honest, inspiring study of creativity, leadership, flaws, and genius.
- **David and Goliath — Malcolm Gladwell:** A reframing of strength, weakness, and hidden advantage.
- **The Road to Serfdom — F. A. Hayek:** A foundational book on economics, freedom, and political philosophy.

WHY THESE BOOKS MATTER

Every book here marked a season of my life. Some came at moments of growth. Some came at moments of surrender. Some found me when I was stepping into a new challenge and needed language for what I was facing. Some were handed to me by someone wiser who saw a blind spot in me before I could see it myself. Some came because I was searching for answers. Some came because I needed help.

Even today, I glance at my shelves and still find myself thinking, *It might be time to read that again.* Books change you the second time in a way they could never change you the first time. They show you how far you have come. They show you where you drifted. They show you what you missed. They show you the next stage of your growth. A good library is not decoration; it is memory and map at the same time. It is evidence of who you were, a guide for who you are becoming, and a compass pointing toward the person you want to be.

A FINAL WORD ABOUT THIS LIST

This list is only a sampling. I built it the way most people build a meaningful list—by scanning my shelves and remembering the books that shaped me when life was real, when pressure was high, when change was necessary, and when wisdom mattered. There are hundreds more I could add. You do not need all of them. You do not even need most of them. The goal is not to conquer a library. The goal is to begin.

Pick two or three books that speak to you. Start there. Read slowly. Reread if needed. Underline a sentence that won't let you go. Write a note in the margin. Let the ideas settle. A book is not a race. It is a relationship.

You don't need to spend money, either. Almost every title here can be found at a local library, and most library cards are free. Many libraries also lend audiobooks through apps like Libby or Hoopla, which means you can carry wisdom in your pocket without paying for it. Reading is not about access. Reading is about intention.

What matters is that you begin. One paragraph at a time. One page at a time. One book at a time. A small reading habit will change you far more than a big reading plan you never carry out. Start with two or three and let curiosity guide you to the next right book. That is how a reading life is built, and it is one of the most transformative paths you can take.

CHAPTER 10

EXERCISE: Moving Your Body to Wake Up Your Mind

The fire was burning even though it was spring.

Not because the room needed heat, but because the room was designed to calm you down the moment you walked in. The waiting lounge at this gym didn't feel like a gym at all. It felt like a private club that happened to have weights—leather couch, stone fireplace, soft lighting, everything quiet enough that you could hear the subtle noises your body makes when it's finally not bracing.

Gene sat on the edge of the couch, leaning forward like a man who didn't know how to rest. He was in his fifties, overweight, successful in all the ways people measure, and tired in the ways nobody applauds. His phone sat in his hand as naturally as a wallet. Not because he needed it at that moment, but because his nervous system expected it.

Jacob walked out with a notepad and the calm posture of someone who wasn't being hunted by his own day. No hype. No performance. Just presence. He sat across from Gene and waited long enough for Gene to fill the silence.

Gene started fast, like he'd been holding it in for months. "I've done trainers. I've done programs. I've tried to be disciplined," he said. "And I'm still stuck. I keep starting, I keep stopping, and nothing changes."

Jacob nodded once, pen poised.

"And don't even get me started on the elliptical," Gene continued, frustration spilling out like it had a life of its own. "I hate it. I get on it, I sweat, I do my time, and then what? I'm still tired. Still stressed. Still hungry. It's like I'm working hard and going nowhere."

Jacob leaned in slightly, about to respond.

Gene's phone buzzed.

It wasn't loud. It didn't need to be. Gene's eyes snapped down and his face tightened like someone had flicked a switch inside him. He glanced up with a thin smile that pretended this was normal. "Sorry. One second."

Jacob didn't flinch. He didn't judge. He waited.

Gene typed quickly—thumbs moving with the practiced speed of someone who answered everything immediately. He hit send, flipped the phone face down on his knee, and looked up again as if he hadn't just vanished for thirty seconds.

Jacob began again. "Tell me what you want most."

Gene didn't hesitate. "I want to lose weight. I want energy. I want to sleep. I want to stop feeling like my brain is buzzing all the time."

Jacob nodded. "Okay. Then we start with—"

Buzz.

Gene flipped the phone over again, this time rolling his eyes as if the device were the rude one. Jacob watched the shift: shoulders up, breath shallow, jaw set. Gene wasn't on the couch anymore. He was back at work. Back in the current. He typed, sent, and looked up. "Sorry. Keep going."

Jacob started, "The reason you're not seeing progress—"

Buzz.

Gene didn't apologize this time. "Hold on."

He stared at the screen, then tapped to call. The moment the line connected, his voice changed—faster, sharper, edged with irritation. "No. We already went over this. I told you. That's not happening. Why is this coming up again?"

Jacob sat still and watched what Gene couldn't see: the stress chemistry surge. Adrenaline rising. Cortisol flooding. The body preparing for threat—while the only "threat" in the room was a glowing rectangle.

Gene ended the call and dropped back onto the couch, rubbing his forehead. "I'm sorry," he said, but it was flat, like an apology he'd used so many times it didn't mean anything anymore. "This is my life."

Jacob waited a beat. "Is it always like that?"

Gene gave a short laugh. "All day."

Something changed in the quiet that followed. The fire popped softly. Gene stared at the floor like a man hearing himself for the first time. "This is our second meeting," he said. "And it's exactly like the first one."

Jacob nodded. "It is."

Gene's voice lowered. "And I've gained more weight."

Jacob set the notepad down. "Gene," he said, calm and steady, "unless you're dealing with a life-or-death emergency, turn off your phone."

Gene blinked, a reflex of resistance rising immediately. "I can't just—"

"Yes, you can," Jacob said. "Because right now your body is here, but your nervous system is at work. And until we deal with that, any exercise plan will become another thing you start and stop."

Gene stared at the phone like it had betrayed him. He hesitated long enough to reveal the truth: it wasn't a device. It was a tether. Finally, he powered it down and set it on the table between them.

The change was subtle but real. His shoulders lowered. His breathing slowed. He looked less like a man on call.

Jacob leaned forward. "Gene, I don't want exercise to be about losing a few pounds," he said. "Not for you. I want exercise to be about lowering your stress and getting your life back."

Gene frowned. "My job is the stress."

Jacob nodded. "Your job is a stressor. But this—" he gestured to the phone, now dark on the table—"is a stress multiplier. You're not just busy. You're interrupted all day long, and your body responds to every interruption like it's urgent."

Gene opened his mouth to argue, then stopped.

As if to prove the point, Gene leaned forward again, suddenly animated with the hunger of a man chasing a solution. "Okay, but I have to show you something," he said. "I found this health hack on YouTube last night. This doctor explained why guys like me can't lose weight. Hormones. It's not willpower. It made so much sense."

His hand drifted toward the phone.

Jacob didn't slap his hand away. He let Gene turn it back on. The screen lit Gene's face from below, and Gene's attention narrowed instantly—searching, scrolling, hunting for the clip like it held the answer. "Here," Gene said, turning the screen toward Jacob. "This is it."

Jacob barely glanced. "How are you sleeping?" he asked.

Gene paused. "Sleeping?"

"How many hours?"

Gene shrugged. "Four, five. Sometimes six. But I never feel rested."

Jacob's eyes flicked to Gene's hand. "That ring—Oura?"

Gene brightened. "Yeah. Tracks sleep, recovery, readiness. I'll show you."

He tapped quickly and pulled up the data. Graphs and numbers filled the screen. The pattern was obvious even to someone who didn't know the app: poor scores, inconsistent bedtimes, a body that never fully recovered.

Gene began narrating it like a report. "See? That's why I'm tired. My readiness score is trash. Deep sleep is—"

A banner slid across the top of the screen.

Facebook: Happy Birthday, Gene.

Gene smiled. "Oh. It's my birthday."

And then he clicked.

Messages appeared. Gene scrolled, read, smirked, typed a reply, then another. His thumbs moved with focus and care—as if Jacob weren't sitting right there, as if the real relationship was the one in his hand.

Jacob let it go just long enough for the moment to become uncomfortable, then spoke quietly. "Gene."

Gene didn't look up. "Just a second."

Jacob waited, then said evenly, "This is exactly what I mean."

Gene finally looked up, phone still in his hand. "What? It's my birthday."

Jacob's expression didn't change. "You disappeared."

Gene frowned. "Come on."

"You were talking about your sleep," Jacob said. "A banner appeared and your brain treated it like a priority. You didn't decide to do that. It just happened."

Gene's eyes flicked back to the screen, still half pulled by it.

Jacob nodded toward the Oura data Gene had abandoned mid-sentence. "You can't out-train poor sleep," he said. "And you can't sleep well when your brain never gets a chance to shut down. Screens before bed keep your system on alert. Then you wake up already behind."

Gene shifted on the couch, uncomfortable because it was true.

Jacob softened his tone without softening the truth. "Tell me what your last hour looks like before bed."

Gene hesitated, then admitted it. "I scroll. I watch videos. I answer emails. Sometimes I fall asleep with the phone in my hand."

Jacob nodded slowly. "You think you're unwinding," he said. "But you're not unwinding. You're distracting. And distraction has a cost."

Gene stared at the phone, quiet.

Jacob leaned forward again. "Here's the seed I want to plant," he said. "When you feel the urge to pick up your phone to unwind—when you have free time, when you're stressed, when you're bored—I want you to substitute movement instead."

Gene looked up. "Movement?"

"Yes," Jacob said. "Not a heroic workout. Something physical that actually lowers stress. Go for a ten-minute walk. Stretch your hamstrings. Do five minutes of mobility. Walk up and down your street. Do something that brings you back into your body instead of feeding the loop."

He paused, letting the phrase land.

"Because right now your phone is your pacifier. And it's costing you sleep, costing you recovery, and costing you the clarity you're trying to get back."

Gene looked down at the screen one more time, then at Jacob.

Jacob stood and nodded toward the door. "And before we lift anything heavy," he said, "we're going to walk."

Gene looked skeptical. "That's the plan?"

"It's the beginning," Jacob replied. "We walk before we run. Small steps. But consistent. We teach your body how to calm down again. We teach your brain it doesn't have to live on alert."

Gene hesitated, then powered the phone down and set it on the table like he was putting something away that had been running his life.

Outside, spring light sat clean on the sidewalk. Huge trees. Quiet streets. A world that didn't buzz.

Gene followed Jacob out.

Not because he suddenly believed walking would solve everything, but because for the first time someone had named the real problem—and offered a replacement that didn't leave him emptier than before.

Exercise Works When "Trying Harder" Fails

Most people think exercise is about fitness. For a leader, exercise is about chemistry.

You can have the right strategy, the right calendar, the right leadership principles, and still show up with the wrong internal state. People may not be able to name what they're sensing, but they can feel it. They feel when you are rushed. They feel when you are brittle. They feel when your attention is split and your patience is thin. That state leaks into your leadership. It shows up in the emails you send, the tone you use, the decisions you make, and the way you respond to conflict.

This is one of the blunt truths modern life keeps proving: you cannot out-discipline a deregulated nervous system. You can't "motivate" your way past chronic anxiety. You can't "focus more" when your brain is trained to scan for the next interruption. Trying harder isn't the answer. Trying differently is.

Exercise is one of the fastest "try differently" tools you have because it changes your body first—and your mind follows. When you move your body, you aren't just burning calories. You are sending your brain a message: *we're safe enough to come down now.* That is why a walk can shift your mood when another hour of scrolling cannot. Screens stimulate, but they rarely settle. Movement settles you because it metabolizes stress instead of feeding it.

Recalibrating Chemistry:The Stress-to-Clarity Shift

If you've felt hijacked, you've felt chemistry.

Cortisol isn't evil. It's useful. It helps you respond to threats. But when cortisol becomes your normal setting—constant alerts, constant urgency—your brain is not optimized for depth. It's optimized for scanning. You start living like someone who's always about to be late, always about to get in trouble, always about to miss something. Even when nothing is actually happening, your body behaves as if it is.

Dopamine isn't evil either. Dopamine is a driver. It pushes you to seek, to pursue, to reach. But when you train your brain to seek relief through screens, your nervous system starts reaching before your mind decides. That "first reach" becomes your default. You can tell yourself you want peace, but your hand will still drift toward the device when your body wants relief.

Exercise is one of the most practical ways to break that loop because it changes what your body does with the stress load. Movement gives your system an off-ramp. It burns off adrenaline instead of storing it. It lowers baseline tension instead of stacking it. It turns the volume down enough for you to think again.

This is why the goal is not "get in shape." The goal is: become the kind of person whose chemistry supports clarity.

Anxiety Lives in the Body

Anxiety is not just a thought problem. It is a physiological state. When your body is braced, your mind becomes braced. You interpret emails more aggressively. You rush decisions. You lose patience. You become less generous and more certain—often with less wisdom.

Movement interrupts that. Even gentle movement—walking, stretching, mobility—shifts the body out of freeze and fight. It tells your nervous system you are not trapped. And once the body stops screaming "urgent," the mind gets access to options again.

This is why so many people report the same experience: they didn't solve the problem on the walk, but they came back able to solve it.

Energy Is Built Through Recovery, Not Stimulation

A tired leader tends to reach for stimulation: caffeine, sugar, screens, noise. But stimulation isn't energy. It's borrowing.

Exercise builds a different kind of energy—the kind that comes from improved sleep, better stress tolerance, and a body that remembers how to recover. That's why Jacob went straight to Gene's sleep. Poor sleep makes everything harder: cravings, mood, discipline, patience. And when sleep is compromised, most people chase quick relief, which compromises sleep even more. The cycle tightens.

The point isn't to become an athlete. The point is to become recoverable.

Creativity Returns When You Come Down

Creativity doesn't usually show up when your brain is sprinting. Creativity shows up when your nervous system drops out of emergency mode and your mind can wander without panicking. Walking—especially outdoors—creates that mental space. It gives you a slower rhythm, a wider field of attention, and fewer inputs fighting for your focus.

This is why leaders often get their best ideas away from the screen: in the shower, on a walk, on a drive, in silence. Those are the moments when your mind can connect dots instead of dodging threats.

THE LEADERSHIP REFRAME

Exercise is not a fitness goal. It is a chemistry reset. When your chemistry stabilizes, your clarity returns. When your clarity returns, your leadership strengthens.

Exercise Is a Presence Practice

Exercise is not a vanity project. It is leadership training.

Leadership requires presence. Presence requires regulation. Regulation requires chemistry. When leaders don't move, they lose clarity—not because they're lazy, but because their internal system gets stuck in stress. And stress makes you smaller: more reactive, less patient, less able to see the "forest for the trees."

If you want to lead from wisdom rather than urgency, you cannot treat movement like optional self-care. You treat it like a tool that keeps your mind available.

The Substitution Plan: Jacob's Seed

Gene didn't need a perfect workout plan. He needed a new reflex.

Here is the seed Jacob planted, and it's one of the most important precepts in this entire book: **when you feel the urge to pick up your phone for relief, substitute movement instead.**

Not forever. Not perfectly. Practically.

If the phone is your first reach when you're tired, bored, stressed, lonely, or avoidant, then movement becomes the replacement that restores you instead of drains you. That replacement doesn't have to be heroic to be effective. It just has to be real.

What to Substitute (Real-Life Options)

You don't need to join a gym today. You don't need to buy equipment. You don't need to "get serious." You need a replacement you can actually do when life is real.

A walk around the block is a replacement. Stretching your hamstrings for two minutes is a replacement—especially if you sit all day and your body lives in that tight, compressed posture of constant work. Five minutes of mobility is a replacement: shoulders, hips, ankles, places where stress hides. Air squats or wall pushups are replacements. One song with your phone out of your hand while you move until it ends is a replacement.

The point is not intensity. The point is interruption and return.

A SIMPLE QUESTION THAT CHANGES THE NIGHT

Am I trying to unwind... or am I trying to disappear?
If it's disappearance, choose a replacement that brings you back.

Make It Practical: Three "State-Change" Routines

You don't have to redesign your whole life to get the benefits of exercise. You have to learn how to shift your state on purpose.

Before the meeting reset: Take a ten-minute walk before anything that matters. Leave your phone out of your hand. Breathe through your nose if you can. Don't force problem-solving. Let your system settle. You will walk into the room less reactive and more present.

Midday interruption: When you feel yourself getting hijacked, stand up. Stretch your hips and hamstrings for two minutes. Walk for five minutes. Drink water. Return with shoulders down. This isn't "exercise." This is nervous system leadership.

Evening unwinding substitute: If the phone is what you reach for at night, give your body a different pattern. Put the phone on a charger outside the bedroom. Stretch for five minutes. Take a short walk if you can. Then read, pray, or do something quiet that deepens rather than stimulates. This protects sleep, and sleep protects everything.

What to Expect (So You Don't Quit Too Early)

If you're like Gene, the first few days may feel oddly irritating. That's not failure. That's withdrawal from stimulation. Your body has been trained to seek relief fast. When you substitute walking for scrolling, you're retraining the "first reach." That retraining feels awkward at first because you are interrupting a practiced loop.

Start small enough that you can't talk yourself out of it. Two minutes counts. Ten minutes is powerful. Consistency beats intensity. And if you miss a day, you don't start over. You return.

That is how a different brain gets built.

POINTS TO REMEMBER

Exercise is not about earning your worth or punishing your body. It is one of the most direct ways to restore the internal conditions where clarity, patience, creativity, and wise leadership become possible again. When your nervous system is trained by constant interruption, your chemistry becomes your ceiling; you lose calmness and vision not because you are failing, but because your body is braced and your mind is scanning. Movement is a practical act of return. It recalibrates stress chemistry, reduces anxiety by shifting the body out of emergency mode, increases energy by improving recovery, and restores creativity by giving your mind space to think in depth.

Most importantly, the win is not a perfect workout plan. The win is substitution: when you feel the urge to reach for your phone for relief, reach for movement instead. Over time, that replacement rebuilds a steadier mind and a stronger life, one small return at a time.

CHAPTER 11

Crafting a Movement
Routine Anyone Can Do

I ran track as a freshman in high school for a reason most kids never have to think about.

I didn't love running. I wasn't built for it emotionally, and I didn't wake up excited to grind out laps while other people got to choose the sports they actually wanted to play. I ran because it was one of the only sports the doctors would let me do. Swimming was allowed. Running was allowed. Everything else—anything with contact, twisting, sliding, impact—was off the table.

The diagnosis had a name that sounded too big for a teenager: spondylolisthesis. What I heard was simpler and more terrifying. If I got hit wrong, twisted wrong, slid into a base wrong, I could be paralyzed from the waist down. The doctor looked at me and said my back was like a rubber band. It works—until it snaps. And when it snaps, it's over.

So I ran.

I hated the burn. I hated the boredom. I hated the way it made time feel slow. And yet I remember the pride that surprised me the first time I ran a mile and didn't feel like I was dying. Something in me shifted—not because I suddenly became an athlete, but because I discovered something that would come back again and again in my life: the body responds to consistency in ways the mind does not predict. A mile became two. The work didn't become pleasant, but it became familiar. I didn't become a person who loved running; I became a person who learned what repetition can do.

Then life happened the way it does. I got older. I got busier. I sat more. And I didn't notice the drift until it had already become normal.

Poor eating habits. Little exercise. A lot of sitting—sitting at work, then sitting after work because I was "tired" from sitting all day. It took no effort at all to come home, sit down, put my feet up, and turn on the TV. Then it became TV with the laptop. Two screens. Probably a snack. I was feeding my brain and my belly with things that weren't the best, and the scary part was how quickly it felt reasonable.

Walking didn't even register as an option. Running certainly didn't. And whenever the thought of movement did float into my mind, tomorrow was always a better day. Today was too hot, too cold, too late, too early. I'd had a long day. I deserved downtime. The little guilt I felt for being tired and out of shape didn't last long, because the next interruption was always waiting. Something would pop up, something would autoplay, something would invite my attention, and the discomfort would get numbed out just long enough to avoid change.

That is when a simple line started looping in my head: a body at rest tends to stay at rest, and a body in motion tends to stay in motion. It isn't just physics. It is diagnosis. It explains why so many leaders feel stuck. Their calendar is full, their mind is busy, their world is loud—but their body is still. They live in their head, and their nervous system never gets a clean outlet. Stress stacks. Patience shrinks. Joy dries up. And then they try to think their way back to clarity.

But clarity doesn't always come from thinking harder. Sometimes clarity comes from moving first.

Movement isn't primarily about weight. Movement is about state. And for me, the most significant benefit isn't a smaller waistline. It is that I am happier when I move. I feel more joy. Little things don't bother me as much. I'm less irritable, less edgy, less reactive. I still have problems, but they don't hook me as quickly. My internal volume is lower. My perspective is wider.

This year, that lesson got upgraded from an idea to an urgency.

Today I am a caregiver to my eighty-nine-year-old father. He's in a wheelchair. As I write this, it takes every bit of effort I have to transfer him from his wheelchair into his bed. It's not dramatic. It's not poetic. It is a real, physical moment where you realize what strength is for. You realize what legs are for. You realize how much you've taken for granted.

My dad is thirty years older than I am, and watching what age has done to his body did something to me that no motivational video ever did. It created a new kind of urgency. Not panic. Not vanity. Urgency rooted in gratitude. If you have two working legs, use them. Not someday. Today.

That gratitude changes the entire conversation. Exercise stops being punishment. It becomes stewardship. It becomes honoring what you've been given while you still have it. It becomes a leadership decision, because the condition of your body affects the condition of your mind, and the condition of your mind affects everyone around you.

Why Exercise Works When "Trying Harder" Fails

Most people think exercise is about fitness goals. For leaders, exercise is about chemistry.

When you are sedentary and stressed, your nervous system stays braced. Your brain stays in scanning mode—looking for problems, anticipating conflict, feeling behind. You become less patient, less creative, more reactive. You can have all the right leadership principles in the world and still lead from tension, because your internal state is doing more teaching than your words ever will.

Movement changes that because it changes the body first, and the mind follows. It is one of the few tools that can alter your internal state quickly without asking you to "think better thoughts" first. That matters because most of life doesn't wait for you to get your mindset right. Meetings happen. Kids need you. Problems land. Decisions must be made. Exercise helps you become the kind of person who can meet those moments with more steadiness.

The Joy Chemistry (What's Really Changing)

When I say I'm happier when I move, I'm not speaking in vague terms. I'm talking about your internal pharmacy—neurotransmitters, hormones, and growth factors that determine far more of your mood and motivation than most people realize.

Dopamine is part of what gets hijacked by screens. It's not simply the "pleasure chemical"; it's the chemical that drives seeking. Screens train quick craving loops: tiny micro-rewards that teach your brain to reach for the next hit. Over time, low-stimulation tasks—reading, deep work, difficult conversations, and yes, exercise—start to feel painfully boring. Movement doesn't give you the same immediate, effortless spike, but it helps regulate motivation in a steadier way, the kind that leaves you stronger afterward instead of emptier.

Serotonin is tied to mood, calmness, and the sense of "enough." Screens are not automatically evil, but when they displace daylight, social contact, movement, and sleep, mood suffers indirectly. Exercise consistently supports healthier mood patterns, which is one reason movement is often associated with reduced anxiety and depression symptoms. It doesn't fix life's problems, but it makes joy accessible again, which is often the first step toward solving anything wisely.

Norepinephrine affects alertness and focus under pressure. Screens can keep you in a kind of information vigilance—always watching, always scanning, always reacting. Movement trains your system to rise and fall appropriately: better focus when you need it, and better recovery when you don't.

Then there are endorphins and related compounds that support well-being and pain relief. Screens rarely offer that kind of relief. Exercise does. That calm you feel after a walk isn't imaginary. It's physiological.

Cortisol, the stress hormone, is not the enemy. It keeps you alive. But chronic stress with no physical outlet can keep cortisol elevated, which wrecks sleep, mood, and memory. Exercise temporarily raises cortisol in a normal way, but over time it lowers resting stress levels and improves recovery. In other words, it teaches your system how to come back down.

There is also something called BDNF—sometimes described as "brain fertilizer"—which supports learning, neuroplasticity, and brain health. This is one reason walking can restore clarity and creativity. The mind often feels sharper not because you pushed harder intellectually, but because you gave the brain what it needs to function.

And then there are the less glamorous factors: insulin sensitivity, inflammation, energy stability. Sedentary living worsens them over time. Movement improves them, often improving clarity and energy even before weight changes.

This is why movement is not a vanity project. It's a chemistry strategy. And chemistry is leadership.

Why "Knowing" Doesn't Change Behavior

If movement is so powerful, why don't we do it?

Because knowledge lives in one part of the brain, and defaults live in another. The part of you that knows you "should" walk is not the part of you that reaches for the phone at 10:30 p.m. after a long day. Under stress, fatigue, and ambiguity, you downshift to autopilot. Your intentions do not disappear because you are weak; they disappear because your nervous system is tired and your habits are efficient.

There is also a deeper truth most people miss: screens solve a real problem. Most screen use isn't about information; it's about state control. People reach for screens when they are bored and want stimulation, lonely and want connection, anxious and want distraction, tired and want numbness, overwhelmed and want avoidance. If you remove screens without replacing the function they serve, you create a vacuum—and the brain refills it. This is why "just stop" advice is so ineffective. It doesn't respect what the behavior is doing for you.

Apps also run on variable rewards—slot-machine psychology. Unpredictable novelty is sticky. It conditions your nervous system in ways that feel personal, but are actually mechanical. Add to that the friction problem: screens are one step. Walking is ten steps. Brains conserve energy and avoid uncertainty. Friction decides more than we like to admit.

And finally, stress and fatigue collapse the intention-action bridge. When cortisol is high and sleep is low, executive control drops. The intention stays. The follow-through disappears. That is the deeper inertia: habit loop plus friction plus state needs.

So if you want a movement routine that lasts, you cannot rely on motivation. You have to design your environment and your routine to make movement the easier choice.

How to Coach Yourself from Screens to Walking (Without Shame)

The goal is not to fight inertia. The goal is to change the forces.

Start by diagnosing the screen's function. Ask yourself: when do I default to screens? What am I feeling right before I reach? What does the screen give me in the moment? And what does it cost afterward? You're looking for a pattern: trigger, emotion, screen, short-term relief, long-term cost. You don't do this to shame yourself. You do it to become honest. You can't change what you refuse to see.

Next, replace instead of remove. Walking must meet the same need, or you won't keep doing it. If the need is stress relief, replace it with a ten-minute decompression walk. If the need is novelty, take a curiosity walk—new route, new street, and if you want a podcast, make it something you only allow yourself while moving. If the need is connection, try a walk-and-call. If the need is overwhelm, the replacement might be embarrassingly small: two minutes outside, just enough to break the loop.

And yes, start embarrassingly small. Mailbox. One lap. Two minutes. The goal isn't fitness yet. The goal is identity and consistency—becoming the kind of person who moves when life feels heavy.

A LEADER'S MOVEMENT DECISION

If you have two working legs, use them—not to punish your body, but to protect your mind, protect your future, and lead with clarity while you still can.

Then adjust friction. Add friction to screens and remove friction from walking. Put shoes by the door. Choose a default route. Attach movement to an existing habit—after lunch, after dinner, after the first screen binge. Make walking obvious. Make screens less automatic. Move social apps off the home screen. Log out. Make it "desktop only." Create a pause. Tiny barriers matter because habits thrive on ease.

If–Then scripts are another way to remove decision fatigue. If I catch myself scrolling, then I walk two minutes. If I get a stressful email, then I do a lap first. If it's after dinner, then I walk before any screen. You are not negotiating with your feelings. You are installing a new default.

Track process, not outcomes. The first win is not weight loss. The first win is the interrupt. Did I swap the screen for movement today? How did I feel ten minutes later? How many swaps this week? Outcome goals often discourage beginners because they take time. Process goals build identity because they happen today.

And plan for relapse. Everyone falls off. When you do, return to the two-minute version. No make-up workouts. No self-punishment. Just return. Returning is the habit. Returning is the discipline.

A Starter Protocol (Seven Days)

You do not need big goals. You need proof.

For the next seven days, do one thing: interrupt your default. Put two minutes of movement in the place where a screen usually goes.

Choose a simple anchor time—after lunch is a good one, because it splits the day and resets your nervous system. If after lunch is impossible, choose the first moment you notice yourself reaching for a screen to numb out. When that urge hits, do one lap first. Walk to the mailbox. Walk to the end of the driveway and back. Do it even if you don't feel like it. Especially if you don't feel like it.

If you need a reward, make it clean. Listen to your favorite music or a podcast only while walking. Don't reward yourself with the screen that is hijacking you. Train your brain to pair relief with movement.

At the end of the week, you are not evaluating your body. You are evaluating your freedom. You are proving one life-changing truth: you can shift state without a screen. And once you have that proof, you are no longer trapped in the old story that says, "This is just who I am."

POINTS TO REMEMBER

The biggest benefit of movement is not appearance—it's joy. When you move, your chemistry shifts: motivation becomes steadier, mood stabilizes, stress recovers faster, and your mind becomes clearer and more creative. Over time, movement doesn't just improve how you feel; it strengthens the wiring and resilience of the brain itself. The reason "knowing" doesn't change behavior is that habits live deeper than insight, and under stress you default to what is easiest and most rewarding—usually screens. Screens aren't just entertainment; they are state control. That is why the solution is replacement, not removal: when you reach for your phone to unwind, substitute movement first. Make it small enough to repeat, remove friction from the new habit, add friction to the old one, and track the interrupt rather than the outcome. And when motivation fails, let gratitude carry you: if you have two working legs, use them.

CHAPTER 12

CAPTURE: Holding Onto the Thoughts That Matter

Most people end their day the same way, even if their days look nothing alike. The house finally quiets down. The adrenaline drains just enough for your shoulders to drop. Obligations loosen their grip, not because they are finished, but because the clock has made continuing feel unreasonable. You sit down and tell yourself you have earned a little downtime, the way a tired soul bargains with itself after carrying too much for too long.

And then the phone appears in your hand like it belongs there.

You can tell yourself it is a choice, but most nights it isn't. It's a reflex—your nervous system reaching for the fastest lever it knows. Screens are the easiest way to change your internal state without doing anything difficult. Two taps and you can stop feeling the day. Two taps and you can numb, distract, compare, disappear, or simply float. It costs almost no effort, which is exactly why it is so powerful. It offers relief without requiring transformation.

That is also why so many leaders feel like life is slipping through their fingers. The most important thoughts you had today—your best insights, your clearest convictions, the small warnings, the creative sparks—do not survive in a distracted mind. They evaporate. Tomorrow arrives, you are back in motion, and what could have shaped your life becomes another thought you almost had.

This is why the next part of the PRECEPT Framework is called **Capture**. Capture is how you stop losing what matters. Capture is how you turn experience into wisdom. Capture is how you stop merely getting through the day and start building a life on purpose.

The Night Ritual I Never Forgot

There is an image I carry in my mind that I can return to anytime I want to remember what capture looks like when it is lived, not theorized. It is late, but not dramatic late—just the end-of-the-day late when the world finally stops demanding. The noise is off. The performance is over. The air feels softer, like the room itself can breathe again.

A small lamp throws warm light across a couch and a coffee table. It is the kind of light that doesn't blast you awake; it lowers the volume. A mug sits nearby, tea still steaming faintly, the smell gentle and familiar. Nothing about the scene is fancy, and that is part of the point. The room isn't trying to impress anyone. It is simply signaling to the body, in quiet ways, that the day is done and it is safe to come down.

On the couch sits a woman in pajamas, makeup washed away, hair pulled back without ceremony. She looks like someone who has given her best energy away all day and is finally returning to herself. There is fatigue in her face, but there is also something else—steadiness. The phone is nowhere in her hands. The television is not running in the background. There is no ambient noise filling the silence just to avoid having to hear her own thoughts.

Across her lap is a hardbound journal, open like a door. The cover has weight to it, like something made to last. The pages are thick enough that ink won't bleed through, and the pen moves in steady lines that look nothing like the frantic tapping of a screen. She pauses sometimes, not because she is distracted, but because she is listening. She is thinking. She is letting the right thoughts rise to the surface instead of letting the loudest thoughts win.

What struck me was not that she journaled. What struck me was what the habit said about her.

This wasn't a productivity trick. It wasn't the latest self-improvement trend. It was leadership. She lives in a world that moves faster than most people can think, and she has learned how to keep her mind from being stolen by that speed.

She is in high demand as a creative director. Her work has been part of viral moments most people have seen without ever knowing who built them. She has helped drive brand growth through audience-first storytelling, influencer-driven campaigns, and content strategy that doesn't just earn views—it changes outcomes. The numbers attached to her career sound exaggerated until you see them in the wild: billions of views, millions in revenue, Fortune 500 campaigns, major entertainment brands, and celebrities speaking lines she wrote.

I have watched her handle pressure like it was ordinary. At a recent event, a top celebrity didn't want to speak and missed a flight. Chaos started to ripple through the room, the kind that makes people scramble and spin and look for someone else to blame. She stepped into the moment with a calm competence that turned panic into order. There was no drama, no frantic performance. She simply did what needed doing, the way capable people do.

I have heard people talk about her mind the way people talk about rare things. When she was in high school, I once heard someone say—with a straight face—that she was the smartest person he knew. Not the smartest high school kid. The smartest person. Period. It sounded like hyperbole at the time, but the years have a way of proving which compliments were empty and which ones were simply early.

And yet, at the end of the day—when she could disappear into the same dopamine loops everyone else disappears into—she closes the door on the noise and picks up a pen.

She captures.

Because she knows something most people never learn: if you don't capture the thoughts that matter, you will lose them. I remember watching her write and thinking, *This is why she wins. This is why she keeps getting better.* She doesn't just live her days. She processes them. She turns them into insight. She doesn't let her mind get stolen by distraction. She retrieves her life in ink.

Then the thought that had been sitting quietly behind everything else finally came forward with its own kind of weight. This woman wasn't someone I met at a conference. She wasn't a case study I read online. She wasn't a celebrity I was name-dropping to make a point. She is my daughter.

Her name is Morgan.

Watching her capture her day, night after night, gave me an unexpected kind of hope. Not only that she will continue to succeed, but that she will stay grounded while she succeeds. The world is not short on talented people. It is short on people who can hold onto what matters.

Why Pen and Paper Still Beats the Phone

There is something that happens when you put pen to paper. It is different than typing, different than voice notes, different than tapping out a few lines between interruptions. Writing by hand introduces friction in the best possible way. Your hand cannot move as fast as your anxious mind, so your mind slows down. Your nervous system settles. You stop reacting long enough to think, and you start telling the truth in complete sentences instead of half-thoughts and emotional fragments.

A journal also does something your phone cannot do: it stays quiet. It doesn't beep. It doesn't throw banners across the top of your mind. It doesn't drag you into somebody else's highlight reel right as you are trying to hear your own thoughts. When you write on paper, you are building a small sanctuary where your mind can finally speak without being interrupted.

That is what Capture is, at its core: a daily return to yourself.

In the PRECEPT Framework, Capture has four anchors—four simple categories that keep this practice grounded and useful. They are not the only things you can capture, but they are the things that consistently pull people out of drift and back into intentional living: **Goals, Gratitude, Prayer, and Thinking Time.**

We will take them one by one.

1) GOALS: WHAT DO YOU WANT—AND WHY DO YOU WANT IT?

If you want to see how distracted modern life has made people, ask them what they want. Not what they should want. Not what sounds responsible. What they genuinely want. Watch how quickly the mind stalls, how quickly it reaches for generic answers, how quickly it feels embarrassed for even wanting anything at all.

That stall is not a sign that you have no desires. It is a sign that you have lived too long without making space to name them. Distraction keeps you busy enough to survive but scattered enough to forget what you are building. Capture reverses that.

One of the simplest exercises I know sounds almost too basic to matter, but it reveals more than most people expect.

Sit down with a notebook and a pen, and write down **fifty things you want** as fast as you can. Speed matters because it gets you past the internal editor, the part of you that tries to sound impressive instead of being honest. Most people can't get to fifty. They stop at ten or twelve, and then the brain tries to shut down. That's exactly why you keep going.

If you stall, don't overthink it. Prompt yourself with categories and let the answers come out imperfectly. Write what you want in your health. Write what you want financially. Write what you want in your relationships, your family, your spiritual life. Write what you want to learn, create, build, or experience. Write the "practical" wants and the wants that feel like they stroke your ego, because ego-based wants are still clues. They often point to something deeper underneath them.

Then stretch the question across time. What do you want in three months? Six months? One year? Three years? Five? Ten? Twenty? You are not trying to make a plan yet. You are trying to put truth on paper.

Once you have a list, begin turning vague wants into concrete goals. A sentence like "I want a new car" is not a goal; it is a placeholder. Capture asks the next questions. What kind of car? What does "new" mean to you? What features? What price range? What would be "good enough" and what would be "dream"? You are training your brain to move from fog to clarity, because fog is where drift lives.

Then comes the harder question, the one most people avoid: **Why do you want it?**

This is where growth begins or stops. The "what" is often not the point. The "why" reveals what is underneath—safety, freedom, significance, belonging, stewardship, healing, proving something, escaping something. Writing the why down exposes whether this goal is truly yours or whether it is a script you borrowed from your culture, your peers, your family, or your insecurity.

From those fifty wants, narrow down to four or five priorities for the next season. Not forever. For now. The rest aren't wrong; they are simply not the focus. This is where Capture becomes leadership, because leadership is focus and focus is a choice.

If you want a filter that forces clarity, run those four or five goals through a simple framework many people call SMART: make them specific, measurable, attainable, relevant, and time-bound. Most people do not fail because they don't want it enough. They fail because they never got specific enough for their brain to act.

2) GRATITUDE: TRAINING THE BRAIN TOWARD ABUNDANCE

A brain can be trained to scan for lack or to notice abundance. The direction you train it to look becomes your emotional default. When your attention is constantly scanning for what is wrong, what is missing, or what might go wrong next, your nervous system stays braced. Joy gets crowded out. Gratitude is one of the most practical tools for interrupting that pattern, because it changes what your attention rehearses.

Social media makes this battle harder. Even if you know what you are seeing is curated, your nervous system still absorbs the comparison. You end up measuring your real life against someone else's edited moment, and the result is predictable. Comparison doesn't just steal confidence; it steals gratitude. It trains you toward scarcity, and scarcity is a miserable place to live.

I learned the power of gratitude in a season when it felt almost insulting.

When I was first getting sober, things were bleak. Bill collectors were calling. I had no job, no car, and no stable place to live. I remember people talking about gratitude and thinking, *I have nothing to be grateful for.* My sponsor challenged me—not with sentiment, but with perspective. Compared to much of the world, I was still safe. I would eat that day. I had a bed. I had two working legs. I had people who cared about me even when I didn't feel worthy of it.

So I wrote it down, and then I re-read it. My circumstances didn't magically change, but my attitude did. My nervous system did. The problems didn't become the only thing I could see. Gratitude didn't fix my life; it gave me back my mind.

This is one reason gratitude is such a powerful substitution for scrolling. Scrolling often trains comparison and lack. Gratitude trains abundance and enough. One increases stress and steals joy; the other lowers stress and restores joy. This isn't merely sentimental—it is neurological. You are training pathways. You are rehearsing abundance until your brain starts to find it again.

A simple daily practice is enough to begin: write what you are grateful for today, who you are grateful for, and one basic thing you take for granted that is easy to overlook. Then re-read it. Don't rush. Let it land.

3) PRAYER: WRITING WHAT MATTERS, CARRYING WHO MATTERS

Your prayer belongs in the journal for the same reason gratitude does. It forces you to hold onto what matters instead of letting it drift. It also gives your mind a place to put burdens that would otherwise swirl in the background of your day, draining you without ever being named.

Who are you praying for? What are you praying for? What needs wisdom? What needs healing? What needs courage? What needs surrender? Prayer on paper is not performance. It is alignment. It is remembering. It is choosing to carry the right burdens instead of the noisy ones.

A simple structure helps if you don't know where to begin: write a name, write the need, and write the next right step if there is one you can take. Capture keeps prayer from becoming vague. It turns care into intention.

4) THINKING TIME: THE HIGHEST-LEVERAGE FORM OF CAPTURE

This is where Capture becomes a leadership tool in the most direct sense. Many people assume thinking time is a luxury, something you earn after you "get caught up." The problem is that most people never get caught up, and a life without thinking time becomes a life of reacting. You spend your days solving what is loud instead of what is important, and the big issues keep repeating because you never step back long enough to address the root.

One of the best old-school practices I've encountered comes from Keith Cunningham. The method is simple: shut the door, turn off anything that can beep, set a timer for forty-five minutes, and think with a pen in your hand. It sounds almost too basic to matter, but it works for a reason. Your mind will not go deep if it keeps being interrupted, and it will not go deep if you start with a blank page and a vague intention to "think." You start with a meaty question.

Write a real question at the top of the page—one that matters, one that has consequences. Then begin writing your answers. After each idea, put an empty dot. That dot is a gentle form of discipline. It tells your brain, *There is at least one more answer.* When you get to the obvious answers, you keep going, and that is when the deeper insights tend to show up.

When the timer goes off, you do something important: you throw out the bad ideas without drama. You circle the one or two that deserve execution or future thinking time. Then you do the most practical part of leadership: you put the real priority where it belongs, which is not on a hopeful to-do list, but on your calendar.

A to-do list is optimistic. A priority is scheduled. The difference between a wish and a plan is that a plan has a time and a place. If you live in operator mode—racing from fire to fire all day—Capture helps you identify the majors and stop letting the minors run your life.

CAPTURE IS LEADERSHIP

Capture is how you stop living reactively. It is how you turn days into wisdom and goals into calendars. It is how you hold onto the thoughts that matter long enough to do something with them.

If you need sample questions to begin, don't look for clever ones; look for honest ones. In business you might ask, "How would I run my business if one hundred percent of future growth had to come from referrals?" or, "What would we have to do so customers say, 'I'd have to be crazy to go someplace else'?" In life you might ask, "What are the four or five wants that actually matter this year, and what is the true why behind each?" or, "What conversation am I avoiding that would reduce my stress by half?" Good questions don't entertain you; they expose you.

POINTS TO REMEMBER

Most great ideas disappear because they were never captured. Your phone trains quick relief and constant interruption; a notebook trains focus, honesty, and depth. Capture starts by giving your real desires a place to live on paper, then clarifying what you mean and why you want it, until vague wants become a small set of priorities you can pursue with intention.

Gratitude is not sentimental; it is a discipline that retrains attention away from lack and back toward abundance. It is one of the most powerful substitutions for scrolling because it restores joy instead of stealing it. Prayer written down keeps your care specific and your mind aligned, while thinking time turns reflection into leadership by forcing you to face real questions without distraction. When you begin capturing what matters, your days stop evaporating, and your life starts becoming something you can actually build.

CHAPTER 13

Systems for Capturing Ideas, Gratitude, and Growth

hapter 12 made the case for capture. It argued that the thoughts you most need rarely survive a distracted life, and that pen and paper can become a small sanctuary where your mind finally gets to speak without being interrupted.

This chapter is more practical, but it's still about the same war. Because even when people believe the message, they often quit for a simple reason: they don't have a system that can survive real life.

Most people don't lose their best thoughts because they aren't smart. They lose them because they are tired. They lose them because the day was loud, the house is finally quiet, and the phone is sitting there like a familiar sedative. It doesn't ask you to do anything difficult. It doesn't ask you to sit still. It doesn't ask you to think in complete sentences. It offers instant relief, and when you're depleted, instant relief feels like wisdom.

A capture habit lives or dies in those moments—not in your intentions at noon, but in your reality at night. That's why this chapter is a bridge between *wanting* to capture and actually *doing* it. The goal is not a system that sounds impressive. The goal is a system you'll still use when your brain is fried and your willpower is gone.

A good capture system does three things.

First, it makes capture easy enough to repeat even when you don't feel like it. Second, it keeps your thinking organized enough to be useful instead of turning into a junk drawer. Third—and this matters more than people realize—it keeps the phone from hijacking the very practice meant to free you from distraction.

That is what this chapter is about: building something that works. Not something you admire. Something you use.

The Real Enemy is Friction

People assume they need more motivation. Most of the time they don't. They need less friction.

If a habit requires perfect conditions—extra time, the right mood, a quiet house, inspiration—it becomes fragile. And fragile habits don't survive. They collapse the moment the day gets hard, which is exactly when you need them most.

Capture fails when it becomes complicated. It fails when you don't know where to put things. It fails when the practice depends on a device designed to interrupt you. Capture succeeds when the path is simple and the tool is ready.

That's the secret most people miss. A good system doesn't demand that you be a disciplined person. It helps you become one.

One Notebook or Several: Choose What Fits Your Mind

Some people do best with one notebook—one place, one rhythm, one daily return. Their mind relaxes when everything goes into a single container, because it removes a decision. They sit down, open the book, and begin.

Other people do better with separation. Their mind relaxes when each category has a clear lane, when gratitude doesn't compete with goals on the same page, when prayer doesn't feel like it is crowding out thinking time. For those people, having separate journals doesn't add complexity; it removes it. It reduces the mental noise that comes from trying to figure out where something belongs.

Neither approach is "better." The best system is the one you will use consistently.

That's why I created the journals that accompany this book. Not as a gimmick. Not as a product pitch. As tools that remove friction. They give you structure without requiring you to invent it at the end of a long day. They give you prompts when your mind is tired. They give you a place to capture what matters without the phone hovering nearby like an invitation to drift.

You have two basic options: one integrated journal that holds the whole practice, or four separate journals that keep each part distinct. Both can work. What matters is that you pick one and commit to a rhythm simple enough to keep.

Why a Journal Solves Problems You Didn't Know You Had

If you are the kind of person who says, "I know I should do this," but you struggle to follow through, it usually isn't because you don't care. It's because the moment you need the habit most—when you're stressed, scattered, and tired—you are trying to build it from scratch.

A blank page can feel like work when you've spent all day working. A prompted page feels like a path. Your mind doesn't have to decide where to begin; it simply begins.

A journal also protects you from what I call the "junk drawer problem." Most people who try to capture without a system end up with random notes everywhere— phone notes, sticky notes, the back of receipts, a half-filled notebook they can't find, a voice memo they never listen to again. That isn't capture. That's clutter with good intentions. A system keeps your thinking organized so it can serve you later.

And then there's the biggest problem of all: the device.

Capture cannot become a practice of freedom if it happens on a screen engineered to enslave attention. Pen and paper isn't nostalgia. It is strategy. A journal doesn't ping you. It doesn't tempt you. It doesn't interrupt you right when your mind is finally settling.

The Rhythm That Makes a System Real

A system works when it has a rhythm. Not a heroic rhythm. Not a rhythm that depends on having a perfect evening. A rhythm that is small, repeatable, and resilient.

There are three layers to that rhythm: daily capture, weekly review, and scheduled thinking time. You don't have to start with all three at once, but you should understand where you're heading.

The daily practice is not about writing a lot. It's about returning to what matters before you disappear into distraction. Five minutes is enough to change the direction of your mind if you use it well. Five minutes won't solve your whole life, but it can keep your life from being stolen one evening at a time.

If you use an all-in-one journal, the daily flow is already built into the page. If you use separate journals, the simplest daily rhythm is still simple enough to keep. You might write a short gratitude entry, jot down a few names and needs in your prayer list, and—if you have the margin—write one sentence about the next right step in your goals. You are not trying to write a memoir. You are trying to keep your mind from drifting.

A gratitude practice can be as small as three lines. What am I grateful for today? Who am I grateful for today? What basic thing do I take for granted? The power is not in the length. The power is in the rehearsal. Your brain learns what you repeatedly aim it at.

A prayer list on paper can stay grounded and practical if you keep it simple: a name, a need, and the next right step if there is one you can take. That one detail matters because it prevents prayer from becoming vague. It turns prayer into intentional care and keeps you aware of what is actually happening in your life and relationships.

And when you write one sentence about your goals—"Today's next right step toward my priorities is..."—you are doing something more powerful than it seems. You are resisting drift. You are reminding your brain that life is not just a series of interruptions; it is something you are building.

The weekly rhythm takes a little more time, but it saves you far more time than it costs. Once a week, you review your top priorities and decide what you are advancing. You don't need a complex planning system. You need clarity and the courage to schedule what matters.

This is where a line I keep repeating becomes painfully practical: a to-do list is hopeful, but a priority is scheduled. If it isn't on your calendar, it isn't a priority. It's a wish with good handwriting.

The weekly review is where you re-read the few priorities that actually matter, remind yourself why each one matters, choose the one you will advance this week, and then put the next step on your calendar. That last step is the difference between capture and daydreaming. Your calendar reveals what you truly worship, not what you claim to value.

Then there is thinking time.

Thinking time is not the same thing as journaling. Journaling often reflects. Thinking time solves. That's why it deserves its own lane, its own space, and sometimes its own journal. The practice is straightforward, but it is not easy in a distracted world: shut the door, turn off anything that can beep, write one meaty question at the top of the page, set a timer for forty-five minutes, and write.

The trick that keeps your mind from quitting too early is the empty dot. After each idea, you add a dot on the page. That dot is a silent instruction: there must be at least one more answer. It pushes you past the obvious and into the deeper. When the timer ends, you circle what matters and—again—you schedule the real action. The point of thinking time is not to feel wise. The point is to become effective.

If you only do one thinking session per week, you will still separate yourself from most people. Most people live their whole lives reacting. Thinking time makes you proactive again.

Choose the System You'll Actually Keep

If you're deciding between one integrated journal and separate journals, don't over-spiritualize it. Be honest about yourself.

Some people should separate categories because it calms their mind and makes the practice feel clean. Some people should keep everything in one place because one book makes consistency easier. If your system makes you feel guilty before you even start, it's not your system. Pick what makes you want to sit down again tomorrow.

The goal is not the perfect structure. The goal is a structure strong enough to hold your life.

Journals as Substitution: Replacing the Scroll

Here is the reality most people won't say out loud: a lot of phone use isn't information seeking. It's state regulation.

When you're bored, you reach for stimulation. When you're lonely, you reach for connection. When you're anxious, you reach for distraction. When you're tired, you reach for numbness. When you're overwhelmed, you reach for avoidance. The phone is not just entertainment; it is a portable coping mechanism.

That means "stop scrolling" will fail if you don't replace what scrolling is doing for you. You create a vacuum, and your nervous system fills it. The journal gives you a better substitute—not because it is glamorous, but because it gives you relief without regret.

When you feel the itch to scroll, you don't need an hour-long journaling session. You need a short interruption that changes your state. You can open your gratitude page and write what is good and true right now. You can write down three names and needs and remember that your life is bigger than your feed. You can write one next right step and reclaim direction. You can open a thinking page and write a real question and a few possibilities, just enough to put your mind back in the driver's seat.

You can still scroll later if you choose. The difference is that you will be choosing from a different internal state. That is the difference between relief and regret.

A Quiet Warning—and a Promise

Your journal is not a trophy. It is not something you buy to prove you are the kind of person who captures. It is the tool you use to become that kind of person.

Capture is not sentimental. It is not optional. It is a leadership practice. When you consistently hold onto what matters, your days stop evaporating. You start turning moments into wisdom and priorities into action. Life stops happening to you quite so much, and you begin—slowly, steadily—building a life you can recognize as your own.

In the next chapter, we're going to get even more practical. Systems are only as useful as the moments they survive, and the moment most people struggle with is the moment the mind is full and the hand is empty. Chapter 14 is where we build the habits that make capture automatic—so your best thoughts don't just visit you, they stay.

ENGAGE: Bringing Order and Meaning Into Your World

W hen I think of the word *engage*, I hear Captain Jean-Luc Picard in my head.

If you ever watched *Star Trek: The Next Generation*, you know the scene. The crew has charted a course. The decision has been made. The possibilities are spread out in front of them like a star map. And then Picard gives the ship what it needs most: a single word.

"Engage."

Engines hum to life. The ship moves. Once it is moving, everything else becomes possible. You can steer. You can adjust course. You can navigate storms, avoid debris, change direction. But none of that matters until that simple condition is met: the ship is no longer sitting still.

A rudder only works if the ship is moving.

The same thing is true in your life. When you are sitting still—sunk into the couch, slumped in a chair, scrolling a phone, staring at a laptop or TV—you may not feel like you are drifting, but drift is exactly what is happening. We give it kind names. We call it "downtime," or "recharging after a long day." Sometimes that is exactly what it is. There is a real, legitimate rest that restores you. But there is also a kind of inactivity that is less like rest and more like escape, and deep down most people know the difference.

This chapter is about that one word: *engage*. It is about what happens when you hear the quiet alarm inside that says, "The screen has had me too long," and you choose to stand up, move, and bring order to something real.

The Moment You Know the Screen Has Had You Too Long

There is a particular feeling that shows up when a screen has owned too much of your day. It is not always dramatic. Sometimes it is dullness, as if the color has been slowly drained out of everything. Sometimes it is restlessness you can't quite name. Sometimes it is a low-grade anxiety that hums underneath everything, making it harder to relax and harder to think clearly.

In those moments the phone, the tablet, or the TV makes a very compelling claim: *this is rest*. You have worked hard. You are tired. You deserve to sit and not be asked for anything. And for a few minutes, that can be true. The first few moments of escape can feel like relief.

But stay with it long enough and something else begins to happen. You are not recovering; you are numbing. The nervous system is not settling; it is going flat. You are not choosing your thoughts; you are being carried along by whatever the next clip, the next episode, the next recommended video serves you.

Meanwhile, your physical world quietly reflects a deeper story. There are dishes in the sink you keep meaning to get to. A drawer you avoid opening because it has turned into a junk bin. A desk covered in unsorted piles. A closet that makes you close the door faster than you opened it. A basement or garage filling up with the physical evidence of decisions you have not made.

None of those messy spaces are moral failures. They are signals. They are small pieces of unfinished work that begin to whisper the same message over and over: you are behind, you are not in control, you start things you do not finish.

You can sit for two more hours and scroll, but when you put the phone down, the spaces are still there and the whisper has grown louder. Screens may soothe you in the moment, but they do not settle the larger story; they simply help you avoid looking at it.

Engage breaks that spell. Not with a dramatic life overhaul, but with a single act of motion. When you engage—when you stand up and bring order to something, anything—you are doing more than cleaning a drawer. You are reclaiming agency. You are reminding yourself: I am not helpless. I can act. I can change the state of my environment. I can create peace in at least one square foot of my world.

And for reasons that are hard to fully appreciate until you have experienced it, the peace that comes from that kind of action lasts longer than the fog that comes from another hour of escape.

Engagement As the Antidote to Passivity

Passivity is seductive because it asks nothing of you. It lets you float. It lets you stay in port and call it "just getting through the day." In that state, life happens to you. You react. You cope. You endure.

Engagement is different. Engagement requires motion. It asks you to get up, choose something tangible, and participate in changing it. That change might be purely physical: washing the dishes, clearing the desk, organizing a drawer, taking a short walk, repairing something that has been broken for months. It might be relational: sending the text you have been avoiding, making the phone call that would resolve lingering tension, stepping into the room with your kids instead of watching them from across the house. It might be internal: sitting down with your journal, putting your thoughts on paper, naming what you want, writing the first page of something you have been talking about for years.

The common thread is not the specific activity. The common thread is the shift from stillness to motion, from consuming to contributing, from drifting to deciding. That shift is the moment the engines come online. Once you are moving, you can steer. Until then, no amount of thinking will change your direction.

The Recovery Lesson: Meetings Are Not the Same As the Work

I learned the importance of engagement long before I had language for it in leadership. I learned it in recovery.

In Alcoholics Anonymous there are two distinct realities: the fellowship and the program. The fellowship is the community—the meetings, the coffee, the conversations, the shared stories, the support. The program is the work—the twelve steps themselves, the actions that actually change you.

I have known many people who were faithful to the fellowship but never really entered the program. They went to meeting after meeting. They could quote the slogans. They knew the room, the faces, the rhythm. But when it came to working the steps—especially Step Four, the searching and fearless moral inventory—they stalled.

Step Four is where many people stop, not because they cannot do it, but because it requires engagement. It takes time. It takes effort. It requires you to write. It requires you to tell the truth about yourself. Procrastination becomes easier than participation. Vague good intentions feel safer than sharp honesty.

I did not do my first inventory perfectly. I doubt anyone does. What changed me was not perfection; it was the choice to begin. A sponsor helped me. He gave me direction: what to read, what the goal was, what the process would likely stir up, what the end result could be. But he could not do it for me. At some point I had to pick up the pen. I had to engage. I had to move.

The outcome of that work was not a neat, polished version of myself. The outcome was truth. I became more honest about what I feared, about where my ego was out of proportion, about the patterns that kept repeating in my relationships and decisions. I saw resentments more clearly and, perhaps most painfully, I began to see where I was not a victim of my circumstances.

I was a volunteer.

That realization changes a person. It does not erase the pain, but it returns power. It returns responsibility. It returns choice. That is engagement. It pulls you out of the story in which life is always happening *to* you and puts you back into the story in which you have a say in what happens next.

Order Outside, Order Inside

A messy drawer is never just a messy drawer. It is a small, physical example of something unfinished. When you bring order to that drawer—when you take ten minutes to empty it, throw away what you no longer need, and put what matters back in a way that makes sense—something subtle happens inside you.

Your environment has changed, but so has your state. Your mind begins to feel less foggy. You have gone from thinking about change to participating in it. You have proof, however small, that you can act on your world instead of letting it act on you.

This is why engagement functions as an antidote to distraction. Distraction steals agency. It convinces you that your primary role in life is to watch what other people are doing. Engagement restores agency. It reminds you that you have a domain—even if right now that domain is one drawer, one sink, one evening, one conversation.

You cannot scroll your way into clarity. You can read, you can pray, you can think, but even those practices become richer when they are paired with real-world action. Clarity is usually the reward for motion.

What Engagement Is—and What It Isn't

It is important to draw some boundaries around this idea, because driven people can easily twist "engage" into something unhealthy.

Engagement is not perfectionism. It is not obsessing over your environment until every surface shines and every drawer is labeled. It is not a frantic productivity binge that leaves you more exhausted than when you started.

Engagement is also not a way to avoid what really needs to be addressed. Cleaning the garage to evade a hard conversation is still avoidance; it just looks productive from the outside. The point of engagement is not to run from the difficult; it is to step toward what matters.

Engagement, in the sense of this framework, is simple: do one meaningful thing that brings order instead of drift. Sometimes that order is external—the sink, the desk, the drawer, the closet. Sometimes that order is internal—writing down what you are thinking, naming what you really want, listing what you are grateful for, praying through what you are carrying, or finally taking a small step toward a goal you have talked about but never moved on.

The point is not to become a person who never rests. Rest is necessary. The point is to become a person who can move—who knows how to hear the inner sense that says, "I have gone from resting to hiding," and respond with one small act of engagement.

A Simple Engage Practice

If you want to make this concrete, do not start by trying to transform your entire life. Start by practicing one small sequence until it becomes a reflex.

The sequence looks like this. You notice the trigger: you have been on a screen too long and you feel that familiar dullness, restlessness, or vague anxiety. Instead of ignoring it, you name it. If it helps, you can borrow Captain Picard's word and say it out loud: *Engage*.

Then you stand up.

You do not negotiate with yourself for thirty minutes. You do not go looking for the perfect project. You simply choose one small area of disorder you can bring into order in ten minutes or less. It might be the kitchen counter. It might be one section of your desk. It might be the stack of mail you have been moving from one side of the table to the other. It might be a brief walk around the block to clear your head.

Ten minutes is long enough to change your state. If ten minutes feels like too much on some days, start with two. The ship does not need to travel across the ocean in that moment. It simply needs to leave the dock.

Over time, this simple pattern does more than clean surfaces. It rewires your association with that restless feeling at the end of the day. The old pattern says, "I feel off—where is my phone?" The new pattern says, "I feel off—engage." That is how a life begins to change without a dramatic speech or a grand resolution: one small act of motion interrupting one familiar act of drift.

A Rudder Only Works If the Ship is Moving

When you feel stuck, the temptation is to think harder. You replay conversations, rehearse outcomes, imagine scenarios, and somehow the more mental energy you spend, the less progress you feel. Often the answer is not more thought. The answer is motion.

Picard's word works in real life too. Engage the engines, then steer. Once you are moving—even a little—you can pray with a clearer head, think with more honesty, and decide with more courage. Until then, you are the captain of a ship that never leaves the dock.

Engagement is not about becoming busier. It is about reclaiming the capacity to move, to act, and to participate in the restoration of your own life. In a world where screens constantly invite you to spectate, engagement is your way of saying, "I am not just here to watch. I am here to live."

CHAPTER 15

The Power of Small Wins

By the time the house finally goes quiet, most people are already exhausted. The dishes might be done or stacked "for tomorrow." The kids might be in bed or grown and gone. Emails have slowed, but they have not really stopped. Your body knows it made it through another day, and your mind knows there is another one waiting on the other side of sleep. You sit down, exhale, and feel the familiar tug toward something that will not ask much of you.

This is usually the moment when the gap appears.

On one side of the gap is everything you know you need to do. It might not be dramatic. It might be as small as the stack of mail on the counter, the laundry that never quite gets folded, the growing list of projects at work, the difficult conversation you keep postponing, the nagging awareness that your life feels more cluttered than it should.

On the other side of the gap is what you feel capable of doing right now.

If that gap is wide enough, your nervous system quietly decides on your behalf: not tonight. The mind looks at the whole situation—the whole closet, the whole garage, the whole inbox, the whole mess—and decides, "I can't fix that right now." And because it cannot fix all of it, it does none of it.

Doing nothing becomes a habit.

This is where small wins matter more than most people realize. They are not trivial. They are not busywork. They are how you prove to your nervous system that motion is possible again. They are how you teach your brain, "I can shift my state without a screen." They are how you rebuild confidence in a life that has slowly trained you to freeze.

Engagement does not begin with huge efforts. It begins with tiny steps.

Why Small Wins Actually Work

Think about the last time you finally finished something you had been putting off. It might have been as simple as clearing a corner of your desk or paying a bill that had been sitting in a pile. The task itself was small, but the sense of relief was disproportionate. The room felt a little lighter. Your mind felt a little quieter. You walked away feeling more in control than the size of the task should have allowed.

That is the power of a small win. It does three important things at once.

First, a small win closes an open loop. Unfinished tasks are not inert. They occupy mental space. Your brain has to keep track of them in the background, even when you are not consciously thinking about them. When you finish something, even something simple, the noise coming from that unfinished loop quiets down. One less thing is humming in the background saying, "Don't forget me."

Second, a small win restores agency. It is evidence in real time: "I can move. I can act. I am not as stuck as I felt." When you have been overwhelmed for a while, it is easy to start believing that you are trapped by your own life, that nothing you do will make a difference. Completing a small, concrete task is like placing a flag in the ground. It may not conquer the mountain, but it proves you can still take a step.

Third, a small win creates momentum. Motion makes the next motion easier. Just as a ship that has left the harbor becomes steerable, a life that starts moving again becomes navigable. You do not need to generate a massive wave of motivation to get momentum. Motivation often shows up after movement, not before it.

What most people actually need is not a dramatic breakthrough. They need one small win they can repeat.

The First Step Should Be Embarrassingly Small

When people finally decide, "I need to get my life together," they often choose a starting point that almost guarantees failure. They announce that they are going to clean the entire house this weekend, reinvent their morning routine, start a new diet, exercise every day, pray for an hour, read a book a week, and be a fundamentally different person by Tuesday.

Then they do none of it.

It is not because they do not care. It is because the first step is too big. The nervous system, already tired, looks at that mountain of effort and quietly concludes, "Not tonight. Not tomorrow. Maybe someday."

A better path is almost insulting in its simplicity: make the first step small enough that you cannot talk yourself out of it. Not "reasonable." Not "challenging." Embarrassingly small.

Small enough that you can do it when you are tired.

Small enough that you can do it when you are slightly discouraged.

Small enough that your brain cannot mount a strong argument against it because the cost is so low.

You are not trying to impress anyone with the size of your first effort. You are trying to build a bridge between intention and action that your real, tired, distracted self can actually cross.

A Menu of Micro-Engagements

To make this concrete, imagine that instead of trying to "fix your life" at the end of the day, you simply chose one small act of engagement and did it to completion. Nothing heroic. Nothing that requires a full tank of energy. Just one small win.

For example, you could clear one surface: a corner of your desk, one section of the kitchen counter, the top of a dresser. When that space is clear, you stop. You do not move on to reorganizing the entire room. You simply enjoy the feeling of one place being in order.

You could empty the sink or set a five-minute limit and wash what you can in that time. When the timer rings, you let it be enough.

You could choose one drawer you have been avoiding, empty it, throw away what obviously does not belong, and put the useful items back in a way that makes sense.

You could take one bag of trash out of the house, especially from an area that has been quietly accumulating clutter.

You could start one load of laundry and commit to seeing it all the way through—washed, dried, folded, and put away—rather than letting it sit in a basket for three days.

You could walk around the house and put ten things back where they belong. Ten is small enough to be manageable and large enough to make a visible difference.

You could open a closet and remove five items you do not wear or use anymore, placing them into a donation bag.

You could finally fix one small broken thing you have been stepping over or around for months: tighten the loose screw, change the burned-out lightbulb, oil the squeaky hinge.

You could sit down and write one paragraph in your journal describing how the day actually felt, not how you wish it had looked.

You could take out your prayer list and write down three people by name you want to pray for, along with one sentence about what they need.

None of these single actions will transform your whole life. That is not their job. Their job is to create motion and to give your nervous system proof that you can engage, even on a day that has already taken most of your energy.

The Timer Rule

There is a hidden danger in small wins that often shows up for driven people: turning them into accidental marathons. You tell yourself you are going to declutter for ten minutes, then look up an hour later surrounded by piles, exhausted and slightly resentful. The next time you think about engaging, your body remembers the cost, and the "small win" now feels like a trap.

This is why a timer can be such a powerful ally.

Before you begin, decide on a time limit that feels reasonable for the version of you that exists at the end of a normal day. It might be ten minutes. It might be five. On some evenings, when you are particularly drained, it might be two. Set a timer for that amount, and when it goes off, stop.

You are allowed to stop even if you feel like you could keep going. In fact, stopping is part of the habit you are building. You are not training yourself to do a heroic clean-up once every three months. You are training yourself to trust that small, sustainable engagement will be there again tomorrow.

Consistency beats intensity. A five-minute act of engagement repeated most nights will do more for your life than a three-hour cleaning spree you avoid for the next six weeks.

How Small Wins Quiet Anxiety

Anxiety is not always about big fears. Often it lives in the gap between what you know you need to do and what you feel able to do. The longer you live with that gap, the more your nervous system begins to treat your own life like a threat. Every room holds a reminder of something unfinished. Every unopened email represents a decision deferred. Every drawer you avoid becomes a small symbol of helplessness.

Small wins shrink that gap.

When you complete something—anything—your body receives a different message. Instead of, "You are drowning and nothing is changing," the message becomes, "You are moving. You are steering. You are capable of participating in your own life."

This is why something as simple as a cleared drawer or a cleaned sink can feel strangely powerful. It is not about the drawer or the dishes. It is about the return of agency. It is about being able to stand in a space that used to accuse you and feel it soften.

Over time, these small experiences accumulate. Your environment starts to feel less like a museum of unfinished decisions and more like a place you are actively stewarding. The background hum of "I should..." begins to quiet, not because every problem has been solved, but because you have re-entered the story as a participant instead of merely a commentator.

From Screens to Action: Using Engage As a Script

In earlier chapters we talked about that familiar moment when you realize the screen has had you too long. You feel dull, scattered, or vaguely restless, and your instinct is to keep scrolling because the idea of getting up feels heavier than your body can handle.

This is where a simple script can help interrupt the old pattern and bridge into a new one.

The script is short: "Engage. Get up. Do one thing. Bring order."

You do not have to say it out loud, but many people find it helpful to give the brain something concrete to hold onto. The moment you hear yourself say it—even quietly—the old pattern is exposed. You are no longer just reacting. You are choosing.

Then, without negotiation, pick one small win from your mental menu and begin.

You are not trying to turn yourself into a different person in one night. You are trying to practice being the kind of person who moves when they notice drift. Each time you follow that script, you are reinforcing a new association: feeling stuck no longer automatically leads to screens; it leads to engagement.

The Long Game: How Small Wins Become Identity

The deepest power of small wins does not lie in the individual tasks themselves. It lies in the slow, steady change in how you see yourself.

Most people who feel overwhelmed carry some version of the same quiet narrative: "I should get my life together." It is vague, heavy, and self-accusing. It implies that there is some large, undefined standard out there that you are failing to meet. Under that kind of weight, almost any first step will feel insufficient.

Small wins rewrite that narrative from the inside out.

When you repeatedly choose to engage in small ways—when you clear a surface, finish a load of laundry, take a brief walk instead of picking up the phone, write a paragraph instead of scrolling—your identity begins to shift. You stop relating to yourself as someone who is perpetually "behind." You start recognizing yourself as someone who brings order instead of drift.

You will not always see this change as it happens. It becomes visible in the moments when life puts pressure on you. A stressful week arrives and, instead of collapsing into complete passivity, you still manage to do one or two small acts of engagement each day. A difficult season comes, and you notice that your environment does not deteriorate as dramatically as it once did. You have learned to keep the ship moving, even slowly, so the rudder still works.

That identity—"I am the kind of person who engages"—is not built by a single big decision. It is built one small win at a time.

Motion Before Speed

If there is one picture to carry out of this chapter, it is the ship from the previous one. A rudder is useless when the vessel is tied to the dock. It does not matter how well-designed it is, how sturdy, or how skillfully the captain knows how to use it. Without motion, it cannot do its work.

Your life is similar. All of the tools we are talking about in this book—prayer, reading, exercise, capture, engagement, thinking—are like the rudder and controls of a ship. They can help you set a wise course. They can help you avoid unnecessary pain. They can help you move toward the kind of life that actually fits who you were made to be.

But only if the ship is moving.

The good news is that the ship does not need speed. It needs motion. Small, deliberate wins are enough to start. Start with one drawer, one sink, one paragraph, one short walk, one bag of trash. Start with what your tired, real self can actually do tonight, not what your idealized self would like to imagine.

Move first.

Steer second.

And let the accumulation of small, faithful engagements become the quiet proof that your life is not stuck after all. It is moving, one small win at a time.

CHAPTER 16

PRACTICE: Replacing Consumption With Creation

L ance first saw Brian the way you know a habit before you see the person wearing it.

It was the lunchroom, late enough in the day that sunlight coming through the high windows had turned the linoleum a dull gold. Brian sat alone at a corner table with a plastic fork resting on the edge of a salad he hadn't touched. His phone was held low, almost private, as if what mattered was not the content but the ritual—the thumb's steady metronome, the pauses timed like breath, the subtle tightening around the eyes that wasn't joy or curiosity so much as surrender.

If it had been a single moment, Lance would have forgotten it. But Brian did the same thing in miniature before meetings: eyes down, tethered to that small bright world until the last possible second, then the tidy gesture of placing the phone face-down on the table, a performance of restraint.

Brian didn't see it as a problem. He saw it as modern life.

Lance saw it the way you see a toe tapping in an anxious musician: the body rehearsing a pattern even when the person insists they're still.

He let Brian sit there for a moment before walking past. Lance had learned that the fastest way to make a man defend a habit was to name it. Better to watch it. Better to wait until the habit stepped into the light on its own.

Brian had an MBA and the quiet certainty that came with it. He wore it like cologne—never announced, always present. In conversations, he referenced "frameworks" and "best practices" with the confidence of someone who'd been graded on understanding.

Lance, by contrast, had never finished college. In another season of life, that might have made him defensive, but defense is a young man's sport. Lance had spent too many years watching smart people confuse vocabulary for skill. He'd stopped taking it personally. He knew what the numbers looked like when the quarter closed. He knew what the room sounded like when a buyer said no. There were no diplomas in those moments, only muscle memory and nerve.

When Brian finally came into his office, the air between them carried that unspoken difference. Brian sat straight, careful, polished. Lance stayed loose in his chair, as if the meeting were ordinary, as if he had all day.

"So," Lance said, "how'd you like the sales training?"

Brian smiled with the restraint of a man complimenting a meal he didn't order. "It was fine. Pretty common-sense stuff."

Lance nodded slowly, letting the words sit on the desk between them. "Common sense," he repeated, not mocking, not agreeing—just naming it. Then he asked, almost conversationally, "You mastered it?"

Brian's eyes flicked up, then away. "I understand it."

"That's good," Lance said, and leaned forward as if confiding something. "Let's do a tiny thing. Two minutes. No pressure. Show me what 'understand' looks like when somebody pushes back."

They ran a role-play the way you run a test: clean, controlled. Brian handled the opening well. He asked the right questions. He even used phrases straight from the training. Then Lance raised a hand—one objection, mild, realistic.

Brian tightened. You could see it in his shoulders first, then hear it in his voice. He started explaining faster, stacking facts like sandbags. The more he tried to defend, the less persuasive he became. He answered the objection like a student answers a question: correctly, but without any sense of rhythm, without the feel of a real conversation.

He didn't pivot; he protested.

He didn't explore; he justified.

Lance let it go just long enough for Brian to notice himself. Then he ended the role-play with a small gesture, palm down, as if calming a dog.

Silence settled in.

Brian looked at the floor, the way people do when they've been shown a mirror they didn't ask for.

Lance didn't pounce. He didn't lecture. He simply stood, reached behind his desk, and pulled out a guitar.

Brian laughed, surprised. "You keep a guitar in your office?"

Lance shrugged. "Some people keep stress balls," he said. "I keep strings."

He played a few chords. Not showy. Not a performance. Just sound—warm, human—filling the room with something screens can't produce. Then he handed the guitar to Brian and guided his fingers into place.

Brian pressed too hard. The strings buzzed. His hand cramped the way it does when the brain is trying to write in a language it hasn't spoken. The chords were shapes, but they didn't feel like his.

"Relax your wrist," Lance said. "Now switch."

Brian tried. The transition was slow and clumsy. The sound broke apart.

After five minutes, they had something resembling a song—barely. Brian exhaled, a little embarrassed, a little pleased. The relief was real, the kind you feel when you carry a full glass across a crowded room without spilling.

Lance took the guitar back and looked at Brian with polite confusion, as if Brian had just failed a simple courtesy.

"You know the chords," Lance said. "We practiced five minutes. Why can't you play like me?"

Brian blinked. "Because you've played longer than I have," he said. "You've practiced more."

Lance tilted his head, hand to his ear, as if the words had arrived muffled. "Sorry," he said. "Didn't catch that."

Brian repeated it.

Lance nodded like he'd just received important data. Then, without changing his tone, he asked, "If you practiced this song every day for the next two weeks, would you feel good about going on stage with me at the coffee shop down the street?"

Brian barked a laugh. "No."

"Why not?"

"Because I'd need way more practice than two weeks."

Lance paused, looking past Brian as if listening for something deeper than the words. Then he said again, "Sorry. Didn't catch that."

Brian repeated it, slower. "Because I'd need more practice."

Lance's smile widened—not triumph, not sarcasm—just the expression of someone watching a lesson land exactly where it should.

He didn't explain it yet. He simply started playing *Yesterday*. He didn't play it like a tribute band. He played it like a man who'd carried the song long enough to alter it without breaking it—little swing here, a gentle flourish there, familiar but personal.

Brian's face softened. "That's... *Yesterday*," he said, and the tone of his voice changed. Less MBA. More boyhood.

"Beatles fan?" Lance asked.

"Huge."

Lance let the last chord hang, then asked, "Where'd Paul McCartney get his music degree?"

Brian opened his mouth, realized what he was being asked, and closed it again. "He... didn't."

"That's right," Lance said, setting the guitar down carefully, the way you set down something that matters. "No degree. Couldn't read music. Still can't."

Brian started to speak, but Lance raised a finger, not to silence him—just to slow him.

"Brian," he said, "training is a map. Practice is walking. You can memorize the whole map and still never get anywhere."

He said it with a grin, like he was sharing a joke with an old friend. "Common sense doesn't make you uncommon," he added. "Reps do."

Brian had no argument for that. Only that dull recognition you feel when you realize you've been using the wrong key on a door you've walked past a hundred times.

What Practice Really Is

If you have lived long enough to become competent at anything, you already know the truth hiding inside Lance's little guitar lesson. You know it, but modern life makes it easy to forget. It keeps offering you a substitute that feels like progress without demanding the price of progress.

Training can be valuable. Education can be valuable. Insight can be valuable. A good book can change the way you see the world. A great teacher can give you a framework that organizes chaos into something you can understand. But the part of you that becomes skillful, steady, and resilient is not formed by understanding alone. It is formed by rehearsal.

Practice is the part that cannot be downloaded.

Practice is the part that does not care how busy you are, how smart you are, or how sincere your intentions are. It only cares whether you showed up again. It cares whether you did the hard little thing that made you awkward at first and steady later. It cares whether you were willing to be bad at something long enough to get good.

This is why practice belongs in the PRECEPT Framework. If prayer is connection before action and reading is wisdom before action, practice is the moment you stop consuming and start building. Practice is where formation moves from ideas into muscle memory. It is where you replace passive intake with active creation, and that replacement changes your brain in ways a screen never will.

The Hidden Trade Modern Life is Making for You

Most of us do not think of ourselves as people who "consume" too much. We reserve that word for extreme cases—people who binge mindlessly, people who look obviously addicted, people whose lives are visibly unraveling. The truth is usually quieter. The trade happens in small doses all day long.

You have a free moment, and your hand reaches for your phone. You feel slightly stressed, and you open a tab. You feel bored in a meeting, and you scroll. You feel a vague emptiness at the end of the day, and you disappear into a show you have already half forgotten before the credits roll.

None of it feels like a big decision. That is the problem. Over time, those small moments train a deeper reflex. Your nervous system learns that the quickest way to shift your state is to consume. If you are anxious, you reach for stimulation. If you are tired, you reach for distraction. If you are lonely, you reach for something that resembles connection but costs nothing. You are not weak for doing this. You are trained.

Practice interrupts that training because it asks for something screens rarely require: presence. When you practice a craft—something physical, something creative, something that forces attention—you cannot be half there. Your mind has to join your body. Your focus has to come home.

That is why practice feels harder than scrolling. It is not just "work." It is return.

Why Creation Heals What Consumption Erodes

There is a particular kind of fog that follows heavy consumption. It is hard to describe until you have felt the contrast. You can spend two hours on a screen and stand up feeling strangely unsatisfied, as if you ate a meal that filled your stomach but gave you no nourishment. Your mind is busy, but not clear. Your emotions have been moved around, but not settled. You have been entertained, but not strengthened.

Creation leaves a different residue. It may not feel effortless, and it certainly does not always feel fun in the beginning, but it tends to leave you with something that screens do not: earned confidence.

When you practice, you can feel yourself improving. Even when progress is slow, it is real. Your brain receives a different message than it receives from consumption. Instead of "I escaped," the message becomes "I built." Instead of "time disappeared," the message becomes "I used time." That quiet sense of agency does something to a person. It makes you sturdier. It makes you less dependent on external stimulation to feel okay.

It also makes you more interesting—not in the superficial way, but in the way that matters. Consumption turns you into a curator of other people's content. Creation turns you into a participant in your own life. It gives you stories you earned, not stories you watched.

What Practice is Doing to Your Brain

When an adult learns something new, the first stage often feels humiliating. You are clumsy. You are slow. Your hands do not cooperate. Your timing is off. You know what you want the outcome to be, but you cannot produce it yet. This is the stage where many people quit, not because they lack character, but because they misinterpret the discomfort.

They think the awkwardness means they are not gifted. They think struggle means they are doing it wrong. They think the fact that it feels hard is evidence that it is not for them.

In reality, that awkwardness is the signature of learning. It is what it feels like when your brain is building new pathways. A beginner's brain is loud because it has not learned what to automate yet. It throws attention at everything—movement, timing, correction, memory, sequencing—because nothing is trusted. Over time, as you repeat the same patterns, the brain starts paving smoother roads. What required conscious control begins to happen with less effort. This is when you feel that small moment of surprise: you did it without thinking.

That is practice at work. It is not merely repetition. It is rewiring.

If you have felt mentally scattered from screens, this is part of why practice is so powerful. It brings your attention into a single channel long enough for your nervous system to settle. It gives your mind a job that is real, concrete, and embodied. It pulls you out of the endless loop of passive stimulation and forces you into a different mode: building.

The Simple Bet Lance Made

What Lance offered Brian was not a lecture. It was a bet.

He did not say, "Stop using your phone." He did not say, "Become a musician." He did not demand a radical life overhaul that would collapse under the weight of a busy schedule. He offered a small trade that was honest enough to expose the truth.

Take thirty minutes from the screen.

Give it to your hands.

Give it to your mind.

That is what makes the bet so powerful. It does not require new time. It requires reallocated time, and that distinction matters. Most people insist they have no margin, but they have hidden margin in the places they do not count because the minutes are scattered and socially normalized. A half hour is usually there, somewhere. It is just being spent in a way that leaves nothing behind.

Practice is what you do when you decide that your life is worth building, not just passing.

What Should You Practice?

This is where many readers freeze. They hear the word "practice" and assume it means something specialized—an instrument, a sport, a craft that requires natural talent or expensive equipment. For our purposes, practice is broader than that. Practice is any repeated act of creation that develops skill and requires attention.

For some people it will be music. For others it will be writing. It might be sketching, woodworking, cooking, photography, public speaking, learning a language, fly tying, gardening, building something with your hands, or even practicing difficult conversations out loud before you have them. The point is not the category. The point is the shift.

You are replacing consumption with creation.

If you are choosing, choose something that meets three criteria. First, it should be physical enough to bring you back into your body. Second, it should be challenging enough that you cannot do it on autopilot. Third, it should be interesting enough that you are willing to come back tomorrow.

If you are unsure, start with something that has a low barrier to entry and a clear path of improvement. Guitar works for many people because progress is tangible. The fingers hurt a little at first, and then they don't. The chords buzz, and then they ring. You can hear the difference week to week. That feedback loop matters, especially for a brain recovering from the cheap rewards of screens.

How to Start Without Turning it Into Another Failed Plan

The biggest mistake people make with practice is starting with an unrealistic version of themselves. They buy equipment, create a perfect schedule, announce the new identity, and then miss two days and quietly quit. If you are reading this book, you already know what it feels like to start strong and fade. You do not need more shame. You need a system that can survive real life.

Start smaller than you think you should. Thirty minutes is a good target, but it is not the entry fee. The entry fee is consistency. If you can only do ten minutes at first, do ten minutes. If you can only do five, do five. The point is to establish the habit of showing up, because once your brain begins associating that part of the day with practice instead of scrolling, the pattern becomes easier to extend.

Make it easy to begin and hard to avoid. Leave the guitar on a stand, not in a case. Put the journal on the table, not in a drawer. Keep the running shoes by the door. Friction decides more than motivation ever will, and practice is built by designing your environment so that the good choice is the easy choice.

Expect discomfort and do not treat it as a verdict. The early stage will feel clumsy. Your mind will look for reasons to quit. It will tell you this is stupid, that you are too old, that you will never be good, that you have more important things to do. Those are not facts. They are withdrawal symptoms from effortless dopamine. Your brain is used to rewards without effort. Practice retrains the system, and retraining always feels like resistance at first.

Practice as Substitution

One of the most practical ways to make practice stick is to attach it to a trigger you already experience daily: the itch to consume.

When you feel the urge to scroll, watch, click, or drift, that is not simply a moral failing or a lack of discipline. It is a signal. It is your nervous system requesting a change in state. Practice gives you a better answer to that request.

You can even speak it quietly in your own words: "I'm reaching because I'm tired," or "I'm reaching because I feel restless," or "I'm reaching because I don't want to feel what I feel." Then, instead of feeding the loop, you practice for a small, defined amount of time. You can always choose the screen later, but you will be choosing from a different internal state. That choice will feel different because you will feel different.

This is one of the quiet miracles of practice. It does not just fill time. It changes the quality of your attention, and the quality of your attention changes the quality of your life.

The Deeper Point Lance Was Making

When Lance asked where Paul McCartney got his degree, he was not insulting education. He was naming something older and more reliable than credentials.

Skill is earned.

Courage is earned.

Composure under pressure is earned.

Depth is earned.

Those things do not come from information alone. They come from rehearsal. They come from showing up when you do not feel like it. They come from practicing the thing until it becomes part of you.

This is why practice is not merely a hobby in this framework. It is a way of becoming the kind of person who does not need constant consumption to feel okay. It is a way of developing a brain that can tolerate boredom, sustain attention, and build competence. It is a way of reclaiming your agency in a culture that profits from keeping you passive.

You do not have to become extraordinary overnight. That is not how people become extraordinary. They become uncommon the way Lance said: through reps.

A Closing Image to Carry Forward

If you are tempted to dismiss this chapter because you are not "creative," remember that practice is not about art. It is about formation. It is about moving from passive to active, from spectator to participant, from consumer to creator.

The next time your hand drifts toward the phone out of habit, pause long enough to notice the moment. You may not feel strong. You may not feel inspired. You may not feel ready. You rarely will. But you can still make the trade.

Take a small slice of that time and give it to something that grows you. Put it into your hands. Put it into your attention. Put it into your own life.

You will not always enjoy the first five minutes. Beginners rarely do. What you will begin to enjoy, sooner than you expect, is the feeling that you are building something real again.

Not just skill.

Self-trust.

That is what practice gives back to a person, and it is why it belongs here—because a life reclaimed from distraction is not sustained by avoidance alone. It is sustained by replacement. It is sustained by new rhythms, new reflexes, and the quiet daily decision to create rather than consume.

That is the bet.

CHAPTER 17

The Discipline of Becoming Who You Want to Be

The Line That Exposed the Gap

There was a sentence Lance said that Brian couldn't shake, partly because it was simple and partly because it was painfully accurate. Brian had spent years collecting knowledge the way some people collect tools. He had the training. He had the scripts. He had the language. He could explain the product, outline the process, and describe what "good" looks like in theory. Lance didn't dispute any of that. He just named the gap with one line that landed like a verdict: *You don't rehearse.*

That's the split most people live in, even if they don't have the words for it. They know what to do, but they don't do it long enough to become it. They gather information, then wonder why their life doesn't change. They attend the training, take the notes, highlight the book, watch the videos, and feel that familiar surge of possibility. Then the week happens. Stress happens. The phone happens. The old defaults quietly resume, not because they're chosen, but because they're practiced.

This is why practice isn't just a productivity idea. It is an identity engine. Practice is the discipline of becoming who you want to be, not by imagining it, but by repeating the behaviors that make that identity true. It is the long road between "I agree with this" and "this is who I am," and it is the road most people never walk because they keep mistaking insight for transformation.

Knowing Isn't Becoming

Knowing lives in the thinking brain. Becoming lives in the doing brain. You can read about golf for ten years and still slice the ball into the woods the first time someone hands you a club. You can watch sales videos until your algorithm is nothing but cold opens and closing techniques, and still feel your chest tighten when a buyer pushes back. You can read about prayer and still never pray, because reading about prayer isn't the same thing as stepping into it. You can memorize a thousand facts about the guitar and still never develop the smallest callus on your fingertips.

Identity does not come from information. Identity comes from repetition. Your brain becomes what you rehearse, and the reason so many people feel stuck is that they keep trying to think their way into a new life while rehearsing the same defaults every day. You can want a deeper life, but if your daily life is built on consumption, distraction, and avoidance, you will get very good at consumption, distraction, and avoidance. The brain is not judging you. It is obeying you. It is wiring what you repeat.

Once you see that, practice stops feeling like one more item on the self-improvement list. It becomes the method. It becomes the mechanism. It becomes the only honest way change happens.

Why Music Makes the Point So Clearly

This is one reason I keep coming back to music when I talk about practice. An instrument makes the difference between "knowing" and "becoming" audible. You can't bluff your way through a chord change. You can't "intend" your way into rhythm. Either you have rehearsed, or you have not.

Even listening to music lights up multiple regions of the brain as it breaks sound down into melody and rhythm and then assembles it into a unified experience. But playing music is different. Researchers describe it as the brain's equivalent of a full-body workout, because it recruits so many regions at once—visual systems, auditory systems, and motor systems—running in intricate, fast sequences. The brain is coordinating timing, precision, correction, and memory in real time. It is doing the mental version of moving furniture up a staircase: heavy, deliberate, and surprisingly demanding.

That's the point. Practice doesn't feel difficult because you're broken. It feels difficult because your brain is building something it hasn't built before.

What Practice Builds Inside the Brain

The TED-Ed lesson you referenced describes one of the most fascinating aspects of learning an instrument: it demands coordination across both hemispheres of the brain, combining fine motor control with mathematical and linguistic precision, while also requiring creativity and emotional meaning. Because of that "whole-brain" demand, music practice has been associated with increased volume and activity in the corpus callosum—the bridge between the brain's hemispheres—which allows messages to travel faster and through more diverse routes.

That bridge matters because better internal communication tends to produce better external performance. The brain becomes more flexible under pressure. It can hold more variables without panicking. It can solve problems with more options available. This helps explain why musicians often show stronger executive function—planning, attention control, strategizing, and the ability to hold both cognitive and emotional information at the same time without collapsing.

Even memory changes. Musicians tend to store and retrieve information more efficiently, in part because practice trains the brain to tag experiences in multiple ways—conceptual, emotional, auditory, contextual—like a powerful search engine. In other words, practice doesn't only teach you a skill. It trains you to be the kind of person whose brain works differently.

This is where people tend to misunderstand what they're doing when they choose practice over consumption. They assume they're merely "being disciplined." They're not. They're training attention. They're training patience. They're training emotional regulation. They're training the ability to stay with discomfort long enough to produce something real.

The Adult Problem: Self-Awareness Without Humility

Children are willing to be bad at things. They don't love failure, but they don't treat failure like identity. A child misses a note and shrugs. An adult misses a note and writes a story that sounds like wisdom but is really just self-protection: *I'm not musical. I'm too old. I don't have time. I knew I shouldn't have tried.*

That story is ego trying to stay safe. It is the adult version of hiding.

Practice requires humility because it requires you to be a beginner on purpose. It forces you into the awkward stage where you are clumsy, slow, exposed, and not impressive. For adults, that stage can feel like risk, especially if competence is part of how they've survived. Many leaders have built their life on being capable, so the experience of being bad at something feels like a threat. That's why so many people quit early. Not because the task is impossible, but because they can't tolerate the vulnerability of the first mile.

But the early awkwardness is not a sign you shouldn't be doing it. It is often the sign that rewiring is happening. The brain grows where it is stressed in the right way—challenged without being crushed. The goal is not to stay comfortable. The goal is to stay present long enough for the new pattern to form.

Choose a Craft That Creates Depth

Practice is not limited to music. The point is creation over consumption. You need a craft—some form of engagement that builds skill, depth, and agency. Something that forces you to show up in the real world, to work with your hands, to confront your attention span, to tolerate the early mess of learning.

It might be writing, speaking, cooking, drawing, strength training, woodworking, learning a language, or studying Scripture with a real plan instead of vague intention. It does not need to impress anyone. It needs to change you.

A helpful filter is simple: what would make you quietly proud a year from now—not because other people clapped, but because you became more capable? That question cuts through a lot of noise. It gets past ego. It gets past performative goals. It points you toward a form of practice that gives you your life back.

Minimum Viable Practice

Once you choose your craft, most adults fail at the next step. They set a goal, but they don't define the smallest repeatable action that counts. "Learn guitar" is not a usable goal. "Get in shape" is not a usable goal. "Be more spiritual" is not a usable goal. Those are wishes dressed up as intentions.

A usable goal has edges. It has a finish line you can picture. It might sound like: "Play three songs cleanly for my family without stopping," or "Walk thirty minutes four days a week for eight weeks," or "Rehearse my keynote opening until I can deliver it calmly with eye contact." Concrete goals give practice something to aim at.

Then you define the smallest version of practice that still counts. Adults resist this because it sounds too small to matter, but small practice is not about skill at first. It is about identity. The first win is not mastery. The first win is that you rehearsed at all. Because once you rehearse, you are no longer the person who "means to." You are the person who practices.

Protect Practice From Screens

Practice dies in vague intention. Practice lives on the calendar. If you want to become someone new, you have to stop hoping you'll "find time" and start deciding where time goes. A priority shows up on your calendar, or it quietly admits it isn't a priority. It's a wish with good handwriting.

This is where Engage supports Practice in a very practical way. Close the laptop. Put down the phone. Turn off the TV. Not because screens are evil, but because they are the easiest competitor for your attention. They will win by default unless you build a different default.

Then put your craft where you can see it. A guitar in a case in a closet is a guitar you don't play. A notebook buried under a stack of papers is a notebook you don't open. A set of dumbbells hidden in the garage is a set of dumbbells you don't lift. The brain follows cues. What you see, you do. What you hide, you forget.

The Ladder That Makes Practice Sustainable

If you want a structure that works for most people, treat practice like a ladder rather than a leap. Start small enough that you can't talk yourself out of it. Build consistency before you build intensity. Let the brain learn that this is simply what you do now.

You can grow the time as you become steadier, but in the beginning your primary goal is continuity. If you miss a day, do not punish yourself with a makeup marathon. That is how resentment is formed. Return to the smallest version and rebuild the chain. Practice doesn't require intensity. It requires return.

The Deep Payoff: Self-Trust

At the end of that story, Lance gave Brian the line that matters most: a year from now, this won't be about guitar. It will be about whether you trust yourself again. Because trust isn't built by knowing. It's built by doing.

That is the payoff of practice. Not applause. Not image. Not the performance of being disciplined. Trust. The quiet confidence that you can keep a promise to yourself. The calm competence that comes from reps. The deeper life that comes from creation instead of consumption.

Practice shapes identity because it changes what you believe about yourself. Over time you stop saying, "I should," and you start living like the kind of person who does. A practicing person becomes less reactive, less fragile, and less dependent on the short-term relief of distraction because they have another form of relief now: progress, skill, depth, and honest effort that produces something real.

Practice is the discipline of becoming who you want to be. Becoming is rarely a lightning strike. Most of the time, it is a decision you make with your hands, repeated until it becomes true.

POINTS TO REMEMBER

Practice is not a personality trait you either have or you don't. It is the slow, ordinary process of becoming someone new through repetition. Most people aren't stuck because they lack information; they're stuck because they keep trying to *think* their way into a different life while rehearsing the same defaults every day. Knowing lives in the thinking brain, but becoming is built in the doing brain. Your life changes when your habits change, and your habits change when you rehearse something long enough that it becomes familiar.

That is why I keep coming back to music as an example. When you learn an instrument, you can't hide behind vocabulary. You can't outsource the work to a podcast. You can't "agree" your way into skill. You either practice or you don't, and the results are honest. There's a reason musicians often seem different—not because they were born with a special kind of brain, but because disciplined practice trains the brain to coordinate attention, timing, precision, emotion, memory, and correction all at once. It strengthens the brain's internal communication and builds a kind of flexibility under pressure that spills into the rest of life. In plain terms, practicing something real doesn't just make you better at that thing; it makes you better at being a person.

Adults struggle with practice for a reason that has nothing to do with laziness. Adults are self-aware. Children are willing to be bad at something without turning it into a verdict. Adults miss a note and write a story: *I'm too old. I'm not talented. I don't have time.* That story feels like wisdom, but most of the time it's just ego trying to stay safe. Practice requires humility because it requires you to be a beginner on purpose. The awkward stage is not evidence you shouldn't be doing it; it's often the exact sign the rewiring has begun.

You don't have to choose music. The point is not the instrument. The point is creation over consumption. Pick a craft that will serve you—something that builds depth, agency, attention, and self-respect. Then define what "winning" actually looks like in a way you can picture, and commit to the smallest version of practice that still counts. That small beginning will feel too small to matter, but it matters because it builds identity before it builds mastery. The first win is not getting good. The first win is that you rehearsed at all.

If you want practice to survive real life, protect it. Practice doesn't live in vague intention; it lives where time is decided—on the calendar and in your environment. Reduce friction. Put the guitar on a stand instead of in a case. Put the notebook where you sit. Put the running shoes by the door. Remove the easiest competitor for your attention. Not by becoming dramatic, but by becoming honest about what wins your evenings if you don't choose.

And finally, remember the deepest payoff. Practice is not only about skill. It is about self-trust. A year from now, the question won't be whether you became impressive. It will be whether you became dependable to yourself—whether you can keep a small promise, return when you miss, and build a life that is shaped more by creation than consumption. Trust isn't built by knowing. It is built by doing, and it is rebuilt the same way—one rehearsal at a time.

CHAPTER 18

THINK: The Lost Art of Deep Thought

The First Computer I Ever Met

My first memory of a computer isn't sleek, portable, or quiet. It isn't a screen you can hold in one hand. It's loud enough to make you feel it in your chest, and big enough to look like it belongs in a movie set on a spaceship.

It was the early seventies. I was a small boy—four years old—downtown in a big building, inside my dad's office. The air smelled like paper and ink, the way offices did back then, and somewhere nearby a large printer kept hammering away like it was trying to win an argument. In the background, I could hear the steady mechanical rhythm of work getting done: keypunched cards moving through a machine that felt almost alive, not because it had personality, but because it had power. At that time, nobody I knew had a computer. Not families. Not kids. Not regular people. This wasn't a device. This was an industrial creature, sitting in a room like it belonged to the future.

To be honest, I wasn't impressed. I was bored out of my mind. I had coloring books, and I had no school that day, and I didn't understand why adults thought paperwork was important enough to spend hours on. I didn't care what the machine could do. I just wanted time to move faster. That was my first memory of a computer: boredom and noise, a child waiting for the grown-up world to stop being so grown-up.

The Word on the Desk

By the time I was nine, my dad had started his own business and bought his first computer. It was a good season for our family. His business was doing well, he was in demand, and he carried that particular energy you see in a man who is building something real and watching it work. I still remember how excited he was about memory. He told me IBM was selling memory cheaper than it ever had, and he moved up from 8K to 16K of RAM like it was a breakthrough. To me it sounded like a strange adult obsession, but to him it meant freedom—more capability, more processing power, more value. He could do more for his clients, solve bigger problems, build a better business.

Sitting on top of that computer was a sign. It wasn't motivational, and it wasn't cute. It wasn't a slogan about attitude. It was a single word in capital letters, the kind of word that doesn't beg to be liked.

THINK.

I noticed it because I noticed my dad doing something that looked like nothing. He would sit still. He wasn't reading. He wasn't typing. He wasn't talking. He wasn't "being productive" in the way most people use the word. He was simply sitting—sometimes staring off, sometimes looking down at a page, sometimes with his hands folded like he was waiting on something invisible.

I would ask him what he was doing. He'd say, "Thinking."

And when I got in trouble—when I acted impulsively, when I moved faster than my character—he would point to that sign. Not as a threat, and not as a lecture, but as a principle.

THINK.

In our house, thinking wasn't treated like a luxury. It was treated like a responsibility.

The Irony That Should Wake Us Up

Most people assume distraction is the reason we don't think. Phones, screens, notifications, endless feeds—those things absolutely amplify the problem, and I'm not pretending otherwise. But they didn't invent it. Long before iPhones and iPads, long before the internet turned everyone into a broadcaster, Thomas

J. Watson—the man who built IBM—was already frustrated that people weren't thinking.

That frustration is where THINK became a discipline, not a decoration. IBM didn't treat it like a private virtue for unusually reflective people. They institutionalized it. THINK signs went on desks and walls. There was an employee magazine called *THINK*. People carried notebooks embossed with THINK. They wanted the idea to become part of the environment, because environments shape behavior more reliably than inspiration does.

That matters for one big reason: if Watson had to fight "I didn't think" before phones existed, then screens are not the root cause. They're a multiplier. The deeper problem is human. We default to motion. We default to habit. We default to activity because activity gives immediate relief. Thinking takes energy. Thinking forces you to sit in uncertainty. Thinking makes you confront tradeoffs. Thinking asks you to take responsibility for what happens next.

If you're honest, that's precisely what many of us are avoiding. We want the answer without the wrestling. We want the result without the silence. We want the Cliff Notes because we don't want to pay the cost of depth.

THE REAL COST

It isn't that you don't have time to think. It's that you're paying the cost somewhere else—through rework, regret, drift, and decisions made under pressure.

Why Leaders Avoid Thinking

A leader can fill an entire day with activity and still avoid the most critical work. That isn't because they're lazy. It's because real thinking feels like friction. It doesn't give you the quick reward of checking a box. It doesn't give you the dopamine hit of finishing a task. It rarely makes you look impressive in real time. There is no applause for quiet clarity.

So leaders drift into a loop that feels responsible on the outside and hollow on the inside. Something urgent hits, you respond, you feel a moment of relief, and then you repeat. It keeps you busy, but it doesn't make you wise. It creates motion, not direction. If you're not careful, you can build a whole life on reaction and call it leadership, and you won't realize what happened until you're exhausted and resentful and wondering why the outcomes never match the effort.

Thinking breaks that loop, but only if we define thinking correctly. I'm not talking about worrying. I'm not talking about replaying conversations in your head at midnight. I'm talking about disciplined thought—deep, directed, deliberate. The kind of thinking that prevents expensive rework. The kind of thinking that saves you months of executing the wrong plan efficiently. The kind of thinking that makes you see what you've been too busy—and too distracted—to admit.

The Satisfaction of Real Thought

There is a satisfaction that comes from a good thinking session that is hard to explain until you've tasted it. When I have a great thinking time, something settles inside me. Ideas begin to connect. Solutions emerge that weren't visible before. Problems that felt heavy start to feel understandable. I don't just have answers; I have direction. I can see patterns. I can see tradeoffs. I can see next steps. And with that clarity comes peace.

It feels terrific, not because everything is suddenly easy, but because everything is suddenly clearer. Ambiguity loses its grip. Anxiety quiets down. The problem hasn't disappeared, but it no longer feels chaotic or overwhelming. It feels human-sized—knowable, workable, something you can actually face.

Some of the best consulting work I've ever done has come out of that space. CEOs will look at me with surprise and say, "I've never thought about it that way," as if it's intelligence or experience or some rare insight. Most of the time, it isn't. It's time. It's the discipline of sitting long enough with a real problem to let the obvious answers pass, the shallow reactions burn off, and the deeper truth surface. Thinking doesn't make you smarter; it makes you clearer. And clarity looks like brilliance in a world addicted to speed.

Solitude Is Not Escape

That joy doesn't only show up at a desk. Once you build the habit of thinking, it follows you. It shows up while driving, when your hands are busy and your mind is free. It shows up on walks, when your body is moving and your thoughts can finally breathe. It shows up in the shower, when there's no agenda and no audience and the mind starts doing what it was designed to do.

Ideas arrive differently in those places. Sometimes they show up fully formed. Other times they come as fragments—a connection, a phrase, a new way of seeing an old problem. Either way, there's a quiet thrill in it, a sense that you're not just reacting to life, but participating in it. Shaping it.

That's why thinking isn't only a leadership tool. It is a deeply human pleasure. It is one of the ways you recover yourself from the noise.

"Engage" and the One Word That Changes Momentum

I've always loved the old pattern from *Star Trek: The Next Generation*. Captain Jean-Luc Picard stands there calm, composed, carrying the weight of the ship and everyone on it, and when it's time to move he doesn't give a speech. He doesn't over-explain. He says one word.

"Engage."

And the ship moves. The engines come online. Momentum begins, and once there is momentum you can steer. You can set a course. You can aim at something instead of drifting.

That's the same relationship between thinking and leadership. A rudder only works when the ship is moving, and direction only matters when you have the discipline to slow down long enough to choose it. Thinking is what engages your inner life. It creates the kind of momentum that isn't frantic, but intentional. It moves you out of reaction and back into authorship.

Jesus and the Pattern Most People Misunderstand

If you want a model of deep thought and solitude, you don't have to look at modern productivity gurus. You can look at Jesus. Again and again, he withdrew to lonely places to pray. He didn't step away because he was avoiding responsibility. He stepped away because he was carrying it.

Solitude isn't weakness. It's alignment. It is the act of returning to center so you don't let the crowd, the pressure, and the urgency decide who you become. If you can't be alone with your thoughts, you will never lead yourself well. You'll be led by urgency, led by fear, led by distraction, led by whatever is loudest in the room.

Deep thought is not a luxury for leaders. It's one of the primary ways leaders stay sane.

YOUR THINK SIGN

Put THINK on your calendar, not on your wall. If it isn't scheduled, it isn't real.

The Lost Art That Becomes a Superpower

In a distracted world, thinking becomes rare. And whatever becomes rare becomes valuable. If you learn to think deeply—on purpose—you gain a competitive advantage that has nothing to do with IQ and everything to do with discipline. You stop chasing everything. You stop being pulled by the day. You begin to direct the day.

That is why THINK belongs in the PRECEPT Framework. A leader without deep thought becomes a manager of noise. A leader with deep thought becomes a builder of direction. The good news is that thinking is not a personality trait; it is a practice. You can train it, and you can rebuild it, even if you've been scattered for years.

That's exactly what we'll do next.

POINTS TO REMEMBER

Thinking feels expensive because it costs energy, silence, and responsibility. That cost is real, and it's why most people avoid it when life is already demanding. But not thinking is more expensive in the long run, because it leads to rework, reactive leadership, and months of motion without direction.

Long before screens existed, Thomas J. Watson embedded THINK into IBM's culture because he saw a timeless human tendency: people default to activity instead of disciplined thought. Screens didn't create that tendency; they simply made it easier to live there. The antidote is not more information or faster execution, but deeper clarity—thinking that is deliberate, directed, and willing to sit with a question long enough for truth to surface.

Jesus modeled that same pattern in a deeper way by repeatedly withdrawing for solitude and prayer, not to avoid responsibility but to carry it with alignment. In a world addicted to noise, deep thought becomes rare—and that rarity turns it into a leadership superpower. If you can learn to create space for real thinking, you stop being driven by the day and begin directing it with wisdom.

CHAPTER 19

Creating Space for Wisdom

From "Why" to "How"

If Chapter 18 made the case for thinking, this chapter is where we stop admiring the idea and start building a method that can survive real life. Most people don't need another inspiring argument for why deep thought matters. They already agree with it. They feel the cost of not thinking every time they make a decision too fast, every time they clean up avoidable messes, every time they realize they've spent a month solving the wrong problem.

What they need is a container. Something practical. Something repeatable. Something that still works when they're tired, busy, distracted, and tempted to fill every gap with noise. In other words, they need a way to create space for wisdom when life is doing everything it can to steal that space.

Thinking Time Is Not Reflection

One reason people "don't have time to think" is that they misunderstand what thinking time is supposed to be. They say they need time to think when what they really mean is, "I'm overwhelmed." So they sit down with a blank page and a vague hope that something helpful will happen. Sometimes it does. Most of the time, it doesn't. A blank page invites drifting, and drifting is exactly what an overwhelmed mind is already good at.

Here's the reframe that changes everything: thinking time is not open-ended reflection. It is decision-making work. It is a calendar-protected block used to answer one meaningful question with full attention. Not ten questions. Not a bucket of worries. One to three powerful meaty questions, chosen on purpose, framed in a way that forces clarity.

When thinking time produces an output, your brain learns it matters. When thinking time produces nothing, your brain quietly files it away as optional—a mood, not a discipline. And moods are unreliable. A discipline is something you return to even when you don't feel like it, because you've decided it matters more than the competing impulses.

The THINK Block

I like forty-five minutes. Not because forty-five is magic, but because it's long enough to get past the obvious thoughts and short enough to feel doable. If you tell someone to "think for two hours," they'll treat it like a special event that requires perfect conditions. Forty-five minutes feels like something you can schedule inside a real week.

The power isn't in the number as much as it is in the repetition. When you do the block the same way every time, your brain begins to associate that structure with a certain kind of work: this is where we solve what matters.

Here's the structure of the THINK Block, and we'll walk through each part slowly enough that it becomes usable instead of theoretical:

- Choose one to three meaty questions.
- Write them at the top of the page.
- Remove all electronics.
- Sit still and write answers.
- End with an output and schedule it.

Step One: Choose Your High-Quality Questions

The quality of your thinking time rises and falls with the quality of your questions. That's not a slogan. It's a hard truth. A weak question produces weak thinking, and vague thinking produces vague action, which means you walk away feeling like you "tried" without actually moving anything.

Good thinking questions do three things. First, it defines the problem you're actually solving, not the symptoms you've been chasing. Second, it reduces distraction by providing a target for the mind. Third, it forces tradeoffs, because tradeoffs are the heart of real thinking. Wisdom rarely shows up in the form of a clever idea; it usually shows up as a sober recognition of what matters most and what you're willing to stop doing.

High-quality questions that are specific enough to be answerable, important enough to matter, and framed to produce options and decisions rather than opinions. If you have five questions, schedule a few sessions. Please don't pretend you can do them all in one sitting. That's how people turn thinking time into a foggy, self-defeating experience and then conclude it "doesn't work." The method works. What fails is the attempt to cram an entire life into one block and call it deep thought.

Step Two: Remove Distractions Like a Leader, Not Like a Victim

This part isn't about willpower. It's about the environment. Thinking time cannot compete with a device designed to hijack your attention. If your phone is on the desk, you're not being disciplined—you're being tempted. You're putting a slot machine next to a writing desk and then acting surprised when your mind keeps looking over at it.

So put the phone away, out of reach. Shut the door if you can. Turn off anything that can beep, buzz, flash, or pull you into someone else's urgency. If you need an alarm, set it and put the device across the room. Your brain needs a signal: for the next forty-five minutes, nothing else gets to speak.

This is one reason I respect IBM's use of the THINK sign. It wasn't cute branding. It was cultural reinforcement: thinking is the work. We don't squeeze it in as an afterthought. We treat it as something worthy of space.

Step Three: Write With Pen and Paper

Use pen and paper. Not because it's nostalgic, but because it works. A screen invites interruptions even when you think you're being careful. Paper does not. Paper doesn't pull you into a link. The paper doesn't prompt you with a notification. Paper doesn't open the door to "just checking something real quick."

There's another reason this matters: writing by hand slows you down just enough to let you think in complete sentences. It reduces the temptation to skim across your own thoughts. It forces you to stay with the problem long enough for something real to emerge. When you write on paper, you're not just collecting ideas—you're building coherence.

Step Four: Use the Dot

Here's a simple trick that turns thinking time from "I wrote a few ideas" into "I found the ones that matter." After every idea you write, put a dot. A literal dot. It sounds almost childish until you try it, and then you realize it does something powerful: it tells your brain there must be at least one more answer.

Most people stop when they hit the first good idea. The dot quietly refuses that shortcut. It makes you keep going until you reach the better ideas hiding behind the obvious ones. The first layer is what you already knew. The second layer is what you've been avoiding. The third layer is where clarity lives.

This is why forty-five minutes matters. If you stop early, you usually stop in the shallow layer. The dot helps you push through it. It creates a productive tension that keeps you in the work long enough for wisdom to show up.

Step Five: Define "Done" Before You Start

Thinking time needs a finish line. Otherwise it becomes either a pleasant drift or an anxious spiral. Neither one builds leadership. Drift makes you feel thoughtful without producing action. Anxiety makes you feel busy without producing clarity.

So here's the definition of done. By the end of the session, you produce one of these: a decision, an action scheduled on the calendar, or a refined question planned for the next thinking block. That's it. Simple, but not easy.

A to-do list is optimistic. A priority shows up on your calendar. Thinking time becomes leadership when it turns vague intention into scheduled action.

Question Banks That Actually Work

If you want help getting started, don't hunt for clever questions. Hunt for honest ones. The best questions tend to make you slightly uncomfortable in a productive way, because they touch the places where you've been drifting, avoiding, or pretending you don't already know.

Here are a few question starters that consistently produce real answers. You don't need to use all of them. You need to pick one and sit with it long enough for truth to rise.

BUSINESS AND LEADERSHIP

- What am I doing that looks productive but isn't moving the needle?
- If 100% of our future growth had to come from referrals, what would we change first?
- What would have to be true for customers to say, "I'd have to be crazy to go someplace else"?
- What decision am I postponing that is quietly taxing everyone around me?
- What problem keeps repeating because I keep treating symptoms instead of root causes?

PERSONAL

- What am I using screens for that I won't admit out loud?
- What conversation am I avoiding that would reduce my stress by half?
- Where am I drifting, and what would "intentional" look like for the next 90 days?
- What do I keep saying I want, but my calendar keeps proving I don't?

- What would I do if I trusted myself again?

SPIRITUAL AND WISDOM

- Where do I need guidance instead of control?
- What am I carrying that isn't mine to carry?
- What do I already know is true, but I'm resisting?
- What is the next right step—not the full plan?
- Write one to three questions. Put it at the top of the page. Then stay with it. Let it produce real answers, not rehearsed answers.

The Pre-Session Checklist

If you want to make this repeatable, write three lines at the top of the page before you begin. This is the small discipline that keeps thinking time from turning into a mood:

1. What are the one to three questions?
2. What would a good answer change? (one sentence)
3. What will I produce by the end? (decision, scheduled action, or next question)

That checklist turns thinking time into a system. You don't have to wonder what you're doing. You know why you're there, you know what you're aiming at, and you know how you'll finish.

The Habit That Makes Wise Leadership Possible

If you seek wisdom, you must create space for it. Wisdom rarely shows up in the middle of frantic motion. It shows up when you stop long enough to hear what you already know, and then stay long enough to do something with it. That's why thinking time matters: it gives clarity a place to land.

Life won't become less complex. The demands won't magically thin out. But you can become more deliberate inside the complexity. You can stop being driven by the day and start directing it. That shift doesn't require a new personality. It requires a scheduled practice and the humility to return to it.

POINTS TO REMEMBER

Thinking time is not vague reflection; it is decision-making work. The practice is simple, but it must be protected: schedule a block, begin with one meaningful question, remove distractions, and write with pen and paper until you produce an output that your future self can use. The quality of your thinking rises and falls with the quality of your question, because sharp questions constrain distraction and force tradeoffs, which is where wisdom lives.

The "dot" after each idea is a small tool with a big effect. It pushes you past the obvious layer of answers and keeps you writing long enough for more profound clarity to surface. End every session with a definition of done: one decision, one scheduled action, or one refined question planned for the next session. Over time, this habit restores wisdom, because it creates space for the kind of leadership that screens suppress and urgency cannot produce.

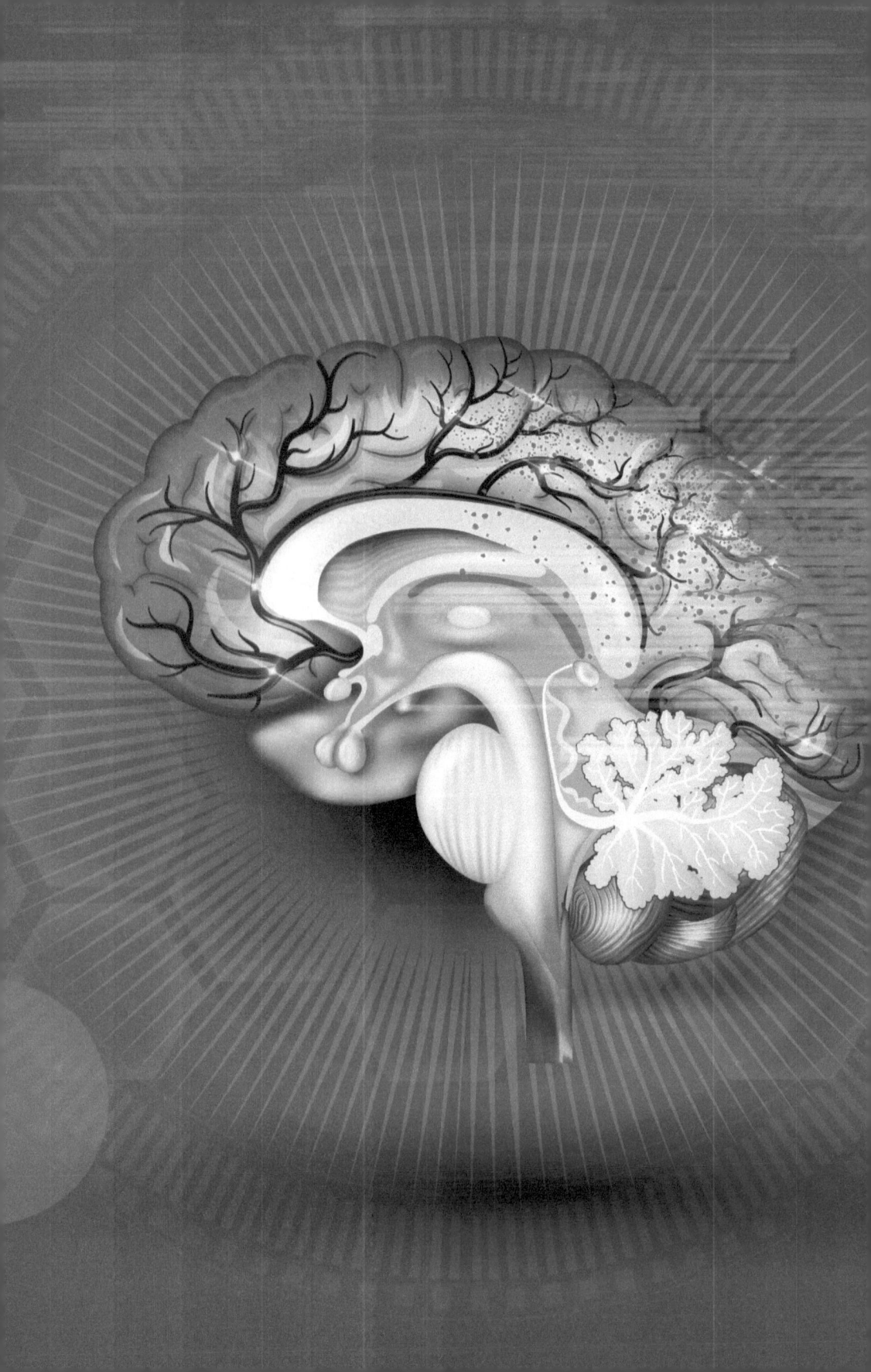

PART III

Living the PRECEPT Life

CHAPTER 20

Rebuilding Your Attention (One Habit at a Time)

There is always an end. The end of a day, a week, a quarter, a year. Endings have a way of pulling the curtain back on what the middle of life can hide. In the middle, you can stay busy and feel justified. You can stay in motion and call it progress. But when the season closes, you look back and the question stops being theoretical.

Where did all the time go?

That question lands differently when you're a productive person. It's easy to assume that if you're getting a lot done, you must be doing the right things. People have said that about me for years. They'll watch my schedule, my output, the number of moving parts, and they'll ask how I manage to do so much. I understand the question, and I'm grateful for the compliment, but I also know something they don't always see from the outside: output is not the same thing as alignment. You can accomplish a fantastic amount and still feel, at the end of a season, that something important slipped through your fingers.

Alignment is what attention decides. Attention determines whether your life moves in the direction you intended or in the direction of whatever was loudest

THE RULE THAT KEEPS YOU FREE

Miss a day? Restart. No shame. No drama. Just return.

175

and easiest. You don't drift because you're evil or lazy. You drift because your attention gets rented out a hundred times a day in small, invisible transactions. A notification here. A quick check there. A "just one minute" that turns into twenty. Over time, those little transactions create a life that feels scattered, even if it looks successful from the outside.

This chapter is about rebuilding attention the way you rebuild strength after an injury: slowly, consistently, one practice at a time. Not dramatic. Not heroic. Just deliberate. The goal isn't a perfect life. The goal is a directed life.

Accountability Is the Real Shift

People talk about attention as if it's mainly a willpower problem. If you just tried harder, if you were more disciplined, if you were "stronger," you would stay focused. That explanation feels satisfying because it keeps everything inside your own head, where you can either congratulate yourself or shame yourself. But it isn't the whole truth, and for most people it's not even the most useful truth.

Attention thrives in environments where someone—or something—is asking you the hard questions. That's why my life is structured around accountability. I have a coach. I have a mentor. I have a close confidant who has provided pastoral care and steady friendship for years. Those relationships aren't nice accessories. They are guardrails. They help me stay honest when I'm tempted to drift, and they catch me early, before drift becomes a season and a season becomes a story.

I also lean on what I call objective accountability, the kind that does not care about your intentions or your explanations. Your business accounts don't negotiate. Your personal financial accounts don't listen to your reasoning. The scale doesn't get impressed by your plans. The screen-time report on your phone doesn't argue with you. Those numbers simply tell the truth about what you are doing.

For health, I've built support there too. I have a personal trainer and a doctor, not because I'm incapable, but because I've learned the hard way that it's difficult to improve what you refuse to track, and it's difficult to stay consistent if you're trying to do it alone. This is a pattern worth stating plainly: people don't change because they know. People change because they stay accountable long enough for a new habit to become normal.

The Year I Stopped Letting My Phone Run My Life

This past year I set clear goals, not vague ambitions. Real targets that required focus over months, not motivation for a weekend. I wanted to become a better speaker. I wanted to get accepted for TEDx and deliver the talk. I wanted to grow my reach. I wanted to lose fifty pounds. I wanted to run for thirty minutes without stopping, consistently. I wanted to write this book.

Those are not casual goals. They require attention, and attention has enemies. The most significant move I made wasn't a fancy productivity system or a new app. It was attention protection. I turned on Do Not Disturb. I started screening calls. And I hired an assistant to manage my email and calendar.

That last one matters more than people realize. Most leaders don't lose their attention to "bad habits." They lose it to access. Their availability becomes an open door, and every open door becomes a drain. People can reach them whenever they want, and because the leader cares, the leader responds. They don't notice what's happening until their days feel like a hallway with no doors—just constant foot traffic. Protecting attention is not selfish. It's stewardship. If your life is meant to produce anything meaningful, you cannot treat your attention like it belongs to the world.

The Overwhelm Trap

When someone reads a framework like PRECEPT, they often have the same reaction: *I want this. I need this. I'm going to start tomorrow.* That part is good. Hope is good. But then something predictable happens. They try to change everything at once.

They decide they're going to pray more, journal every night, walk daily, practice a craft, do thinking time, set goals, stop scrolling, overhaul their sleep, improve their diet, clean the garage, repair the marriage, rebuild the business, and become a new person by Friday. That isn't growth. That's overwhelm disguised as ambition.

It usually ends the same way. A short burst of intensity, a missed day, discouragement, and a quiet return to old defaults, because the plan was never sustainable. The person doesn't fail because they lack character. They fail because they treated attention like a revolution instead of rehab.

Rebuilding attention is not something you do overnight. It's something you install slowly, the same way your body heals: one stable practice at a time. You don't rebuild strength by attempting the heaviest weight on day one. You rebuild it by doing what you can do consistently until your system trusts it again.

The First Habit Is Different for Everyone

People always want the same thing from a book: tell me exactly what to do first. I understand that desire. It's comforting to have a clear starting line. But the honest answer is that the first habit is different for everyone, because everyone is in a different season. Some people are exhausted. Some are anxious. Some are bored. Some are grieving. Some are overwhelmed. Some are over-stimulated. Some are under-disciplined. And the first habit that helps one person may frustrate another.

That's why I often recommend starting with a thinking-time block—not because thinking time is always the first habit you implement, but because it helps you choose the right first habit for your life. It slows you down long enough to see clearly. It gives you a place to ask the question you can't answer while you're in motion.

Use one thinking session to answer a simple question: *What are the three habits that would make the most difference right now?* Then choose the most important one and begin there. If you don't choose deliberately, you'll default to whatever feels easiest or most inspirational in the moment. And that's rarely what changes your life.

The One-Habit Method

The approach I trust is almost boring, which is exactly why it works. Identify one habit that matters most right now. Make it small enough to succeed. Do it long enough that it starts to feel stable. Then add the next habit without abandoning the first one.

When I say "do it for 21 days," I'm not claiming there's a magical transformation number. It's simply a practical threshold where a behavior starts feeling less foreign. You're teaching your brain, *this is what we do now.* You're building the beginning of an identity, not chasing a mood.

When you add a new habit, you keep the old one alive at a minimum viable level. You don't need to expand everything at once. You just need continuity. This is how attention gets rebuilt without your plan collapsing under its own weight.

The Relapse Rule That Keeps You Free

Most people don't fail because they relapse. They fail because they make relapse mean something about who they are. They miss a day and immediately begin the shame story: *See? This is why I can't change. I never stick with anything. I'm back at zero.*

No. Here is the relapse rule: if you miss a day, start again.

That's it. No punishment. No drama. No makeup marathons to "pay for" what you missed. Just restart. If you measure progress by perfection, you will quit. If you measure progress by return, you will grow. In the language of recovery, this matters deeply. You don't measure progress by whether you stumble. You measure progress by whether you come back.

When Habits Stop Depending on Memory

A lot of people assume they need more motivation. Usually they don't. They need better design. This is where habit stacking becomes one of the simplest tools for rebuilding attention. It removes decision-making. You attach a new habit to an old habit you already do reliably, and the new habit stops competing with memory.

Imagine you want to improve balance. Standing on one leg is one of the best ways to do it. You decide you're going to do it for thirty days. But life happens, and you forget. You get distracted, not because you don't care, but because your brain is busy.

So you stack it. Every day you brush your teeth. You don't forget that. You don't need motivation for it. It's already installed. So while you brush your teeth, you stand on one foot. Now the habit isn't competing with memory. It's riding the rails of something already automatic.

That's the genius of stacking. It reduces friction, and friction is the real enemy of consistency.

You can stack almost anything. You can attach journaling to your morning coffee. You can attach a walk to lunch. You can attach a reset to the end of your last meeting. You can attach practice to the moment you feel the itch to scroll. When the stack becomes a trigger, the trigger becomes automatic. And automatic is what you want, because attention collapses when life is stressful, but systems keep working.

A Directed Life Is the Goal

The goal of PRECEPT is not for you to become a monk with flawless habits. The goal is for you to stop living in reaction. To rebuild your attention until you can choose again. When your attention begins to return, your days start to feel different. Not necessarily easier, but cleaner. More aligned. Less scattered. Less regretful.

You begin to feel what real intention feels like: peace. Not the peace of having nothing to do, but the peace of knowing you are doing what matters.

An Invitation for This Week

If you only do one thing this week, don't try to overhaul your life. Schedule one thinking-time block. Forty-five minutes. Pen and paper. No phone. Write one question at the top of the page: *What are the three habits that would make the most difference in my life right now?* Then write until you have an answer you trust.

When you're done, choose one habit. Make it embarrassingly small. Do it tomorrow. And if you miss a day, start again.

Because rebuilding attention is not about proving you're impressive. It's about rebuilding trust with yourself, one habit at a time.

POINTS TO REMEMBER

Attention is not only a discipline problem; it is often an accountability problem. People change when they stay accountable long enough for new habits to become normal, and both trusted relationships and objective metrics help tell the truth when excuses feel persuasive. Even highly productive people can suffer from misalignment, doing a lot while missing what matters most, because attention follows what is loud and easy unless it is protected.

Rebuilding attention is closer to rehab than revolution. It works best when you install one habit until it becomes stable, then add the next without abandoning the first. The relapse rule is simple and freeing: if you miss a day, start again. Habit stacking reduces friction by attaching new habits to existing routines, turning change from a memory problem into a design solution. Over time, this slow, consistent approach restores direction, peace, and self-trust—the kind that comes from returning, not performing.

CHAPTER 21

The Leadership Impact

The Question Most People Answer Too Quickly

Are you a leader?

Most people answer that question too fast, and they answer it by picturing a certain kind of person. They picture a CEO or a coach, a pastor or a politician, a manager with direct reports, or someone standing at the front of a room with a microphone. If that isn't your life, it's easy to shrug and say, "No, I'm not a leader," and move on.

But leadership doesn't start with a title. Leadership starts with influence. Influence is simply the ability to affect what happens next—what people think, how they feel, what they do, what they tolerate, and what they become. By that definition, leadership isn't rare. It's everywhere. It's in homes and friendships, in workplaces and neighborhoods, in how you handle pressure, how you speak when you're tired, and what you do when nobody is clapping.

The first person you lead every single day is yourself. You lead your attention. You lead your habits. You lead your reactions. You lead what you consume, what you avoid, what you prioritize, and what you postpone. And whether you realize it or not, the way you lead yourself leaks into the lives of the people around you. It shows up in your tone, your consistency, your patience, your decision-making, your follow-through, your presence, and your trustworthiness.

Leadership expands outward in a predictable order: self, then family, then team, then organization, then community. That sequence matters, not because one circle is more "important," but because influence multiplies. If your internal world is chaotic, your outer world eventually reflects it. If your attention is scattered, the people who depend on you pay the price. If your life is calm, consistent, and anchored, other people borrow stability from you without you even trying.

So yes—if you have a spouse, a child, a friend, a team, a customer, a coworker, a neighbor, or anyone watching you, depending on you, or taking cues from you, then you are a leader. The only question is what kind.

THE ORDER THAT WORKS

You can't give away what you don't have. Lead yourself first, not because you're the center of the universe, but because you're the first environment other people have to live inside.

The Leadership Vacuum We Can All Feel

We are living in a leadership vacuum. Not because we lack information, and not because we lack access to experts. We have podcasts and books, certifications and courses, frameworks and "best practices." We can learn from the smartest people in the world while sitting on a couch with a phone in our hand.

What we have less of is embodied clarity.

We have a shortage of people who can stay present under pressure. People who can hold a steady heading when the winds shift. People who can think instead of react. People who can remain consistent long enough for trust to grow. People who can resist being hijacked by every new fear, outrage, trend, or "game-changing" idea.

And here is the uncomfortable truth: when society loses embodied leadership, people start following whoever feels certain. Certainty attracts followers even when it's detached from wisdom. Confidence attracts attention even when it isn't grounded in character. A loud voice attracts a crowd even when it isn't leading anyone anywhere.

That's why the people who unhijack themselves stand out so quickly. They don't need to be the loudest. They don't need to perform. They don't need to dominate the room. Calm is rare now. Consistency is rare now. Integrity is rare now. And the person who becomes steady becomes influential, often without trying, because everyone is tired of being tossed around.

If you take back your attention, you take back your life. But you also take back something larger. You take back your leadership.

You Can't Give Away What You Don't Have

This may be one of the most important truths in the entire book: you can't give away what you don't have.

A distracted leader cannot teach presence. A reactive leader cannot teach emotional maturity. A scattered leader cannot teach clarity. A leader who cannot manage their own inputs cannot train a team to focus. And this is where many leaders get stuck, because it is far easier to export change than to embody it.

It is easier to buy a book and hand it to your team than to let the book confront you. It is easier to send an article, forward a podcast, post a quote, and announce a new initiative than it is to practice a new way of living. It is easier to say, "Everyone needs to improve," than to admit, "I need to improve first."

This is one of the oldest leadership temptations: treating the people around you like the problem you need to fix. You might not call it that, but it shows up in the tone many frustrated leaders carry. If they would execute, we'd be fine. If they would communicate better, we'd be fine. If they were more motivated, we'd be fine. If they would stop making mistakes, we'd be fine.

But the leadership breakthrough rarely begins with the cast. It begins with the director. The leader who wants others to change has to become the kind of person who can carry the change.

Distracted Leadership Feels Like Whiplash

A distracted leader often presents as sincere, passionate, fast-moving, energized. They can walk into a Monday meeting with real conviction. They can declare a priority with intensity. They can motivate people and create urgency. They can rally the troops, and for a moment, everyone feels hopeful.

And then by Friday, everything has changed.

A pithy quote on Instagram "unlocked" a new idea. A viral clip from YouTube "changed everything." A LinkedIn post from a respected leader introduced a new framework. A podcast episode reframed the problem. A late-night scroll produced a new fear, a new enemy, or a new opportunity. The leader doesn't always see the pattern because it feels like learning. It feels like growth. It feels like agility. They believe they're staying informed and moving fast.

But the team experiences it differently. The team experiences whiplash.

Whiplash is not a minor inconvenience. Whiplash destroys trust. It trains people to stop taking priorities seriously. It forces them to protect themselves by waiting. They learn to delay commitment until the leader's mood stabilizes. They become cautious, not because they're lazy, but because the environment has taught them that urgency is temporary and direction is unstable.

This is why distracted leaders struggle to build velocity, and velocity is everything.

Harbor Waves and Forward Motion

Imagine leadership like a boat.

When a boat is stuck in the harbor with its anchor down, it gets tossed by the waves. Every wave pushes it around. It drifts. It jerks. It feels unstable. The passengers get seasick. That's what it feels like to be on a team led by a distracted leader. Multiple inputs are hitting the leader's mind at once—email, texts, Slack, headlines, videos, notifications, constant information. The brain becomes an ocean of competing waves, and the leader becomes a small boat being thrown around.

The passengers—your family, your team, your organization—feel the motion. And seasick passengers don't become brave builders. They look for relief. They look for something to stabilize them. Increasingly, people cope with stress by picking up a screen. The very thing that created the waves becomes the thing they reach for to feel better, like drinking saltwater to satisfy thirst.

Now picture a different boat. A boat with its sail up and a heading set is not getting tossed by the waves. It is cutting through them. It has forward motion. It has purpose. It has velocity. It may still feel the storm, but it moves through it.

That's what happens when a leader develops habits that generate momentum. Velocity stabilizes. And this is why distraction is so dangerous. Distraction doesn't just steal time; it steals velocity. It keeps people stuck in the harbor—endlessly anticipating the journey, talking about the journey, posting about the journey, admiring other people's journeys, collecting motivational quotes about the journey—without ever leaving port.

When your habits change and you substitute screen time for thinking time, when you raise the sail, leave the harbor, and start moving, you feel better. Not because everything is perfect, but because you are progressing. You are no longer merely anticipating. You are doing. You are on a journey, not dreaming of one.

Progress creates a healthy kind of pride—the kind that comes from becoming the kind of person who can do hard things. Over time, you develop a new default. You set a better sail. You keep a heading. You measure movement. You see progress. And each time you return to the practices, it becomes easier to pull up the anchor and leave port again.

This is what the PRECEPT Framework is designed to produce. Not a burst of inspiration, but an embodied way of living that creates steady forward motion.

What Your Leadership Creates for Other People

When a leader has velocity—when they're living with presence, clarity, and consistency—something changes for everyone around them. People experience stability because the ground stops shifting under their feet. They experience clarity because priorities hold long enough to execute. They experience trust because words begin matching actions again.

They also experience something many people don't realize they're starving for: emotional safety. The ability to have honest conversations without punishment. The freedom to admit a mistake without being shamed. The confidence to take initiative without fear of being blindsided by a sudden change of direction.

If you want a simple way to measure leadership impact, don't start with speeches or slogans. Start with the environment your inner life creates. Your habits become a culture. Your attention becomes a signal to everyone else about what deserves attention. Leadership is not primarily what you say. It's what you create.

And the impact doesn't stop at work. It shows up at home. A distracted parent can be physically present and emotionally absent. A distracted spouse can be in the same room but unreachable. A distracted leader can be surrounded by people and still be alone—not because they don't care, but because their attention has been outsourced.

Presence is leadership in the most practical sense. When you are present, you shape the room. When you are absent, the room shapes itself, usually not in the way you intended.

The Highest Achievement: Teaching People to Lead Themselves

One of the greatest achievements of a leader is not controlling people. It's helping them lead themselves.

A strong leader does not create dependence. A strong leader creates capability. They're not just steering the ship; they're training other people to become sailors. They're teaching them how to set a sail, how to find a heading, how to read the wind, how to stay steady, and how to move forward even when conditions are imperfect.

Here's the uncomfortable part: a leader who doesn't know how to set their own sail gets frustrated when others can't set theirs. They demand focus they don't model. They demand discipline they don't practice. They demand maturity they don't embody. They demand calm while living in chaos. They demand consistency while changing direction weekly. They demand execution while interrupting flow.

The team isn't confused because they're incompetent. The team is confused because the leader is inconsistent. Fragmentation spreads. What the leader tolerates becomes normal. What the leader reacts to becomes urgent. What the leader repeatedly fails to do becomes permission for everyone else to drift.

This is why leadership must begin with self—not as a motivational slogan, but as a structural reality. The leader is always teaching, even when they think they're not.

Ancient Wisdom: The Log, the Speck, and Clear Sight

Two illustrations capture this better than any modern leadership theory.

The first is ancient, and it cuts straight through the human tendency to fix everyone else first. Jesus asks a question that exposes how easy it is to become an expert on other people's flaws while remaining blind to your own. He says, in essence, *Why are you so focused on the speck in someone else's eye while ignoring the log in your own?* (Matthew 7:3). The point isn't that you should never help anyone. The point is sequence and clarity. Remove the log first. Then you will see clearly enough to help with the speck.

That's leadership. Not the performance of correction, but the discipline of self-confrontation that gives you the right kind of vision. When you do your own work first, you stop projecting, blaming, and reacting. You start seeing.

The Oxygen Mask and the Order That Matters

The second illustration is familiar to anyone who has flown. You've heard it in the safety briefing so many times it can feel like background noise: put the oxygen mask on yourself first, then put the mask on your child. That isn't selfishness. That is sequence.

If you pass out, you can't help anyone. If you can't breathe, you can't lead. If you are hijacked, you can't stabilize others. If you are drowning in distraction, you can't teach someone else to swim. Leadership is not about being perfect. It's about being honest enough to work the right order.

Self first. Then family. Then team. Then organization. Then community.

Not because you matter more than others, but because you can't give away what you don't have.

Prison Advice and an Escape Story

There's one more picture I want to leave you with because it explains why so much leadership advice falls flat.

Imagine someone sitting in a prison cell telling the other inmates all about escape. They may be sincere. They may be intelligent. They may even have good information. But there is a credibility gap. Something in us knows it immediately: if you really know the way out, why are you still here?

Now imagine someone who escaped and came back to tell the story. Not just *here's the plan,* but *here's who I became on the other side of the walls.* That person doesn't need to dominate the room. Their presence carries authority because they are living evidence.

That's the kind of leadership that changes people. A leader can't lead people out of distraction while still being enslaved by it. You can't teach someone to unhijack their attention while your own attention is constantly hijacked. You can't call people into maturity while refusing the discomfort of growth yourself.

But the moment you begin to escape—when you begin to practice the PRECEPT Framework not as a concept but as a way of living—your leadership changes. You may not notice it at first, but other people will. In a leadership vacuum, embodied clarity becomes a lighthouse. And lighthouses don't chase ships. They stand steady, and ships find them.

An Invitation to Lead Yourself First

If you're reading this and thinking, "I don't feel like a leader," let me bring you back to the beginning. Leadership is influence. You are influencing someone. You are influencing yourself. You are influencing the people closest to you with your habits and your attention.

The question isn't whether you lead. The question is whether you are willing to lead yourself first.

It is easy to keep your sail down, your anchor in, and your phone in your hand while you talk about the journey. It is harder to leave port. It is harder to set a heading, raise the sail, and develop velocity. But that's where the relief is. That's where peace is. That's where trust is rebuilt—first inside you, and then around you.

When that begins to happen, you become the kind of leader people want to follow, not because you demand it, but because you are no longer being tossed by the waves. You become steady. You become consistent. You become present. And once you've learned to set your sail, you can help other people set theirs.

That is leadership. That is impact.

POINTS TO REMEMBER

Leadership begins with influence, not a title, and the first person you lead every day is yourself—your attention, habits, reactions, and priorities. In a leadership vacuum, embodied clarity stands out because calm, consistency, and integrity have become rare. You can't give away what you don't have, which is why leaders who want change in others must begin by embodying it themselves.

Distracted leadership creates whiplash that destroys trust and slows execution, while velocity stabilizes people the way a boat with a heading cuts through waves instead of being tossed in the harbor. Ancient wisdom captures the sequence: Jesus warns against obsessing over the speck in someone else's eye while ignoring the log in your own (Matthew 7:3), because clear sight comes after self-work, not before it. The oxygen-mask principle applies here as well: if you don't regain your own air—your presence, clarity, and stability—you won't have enough to give away.

CHAPTER 22

Your New Identity

The Question Most People Avoid

There is a question most people avoid—not because it is complicated, but because it is personal. It doesn't care what you meant to do, what you hoped to do, or what you promised yourself you would do next week. It asks for something more honest than intention, and more revealing than aspiration.

Who are you becoming?

Not what do you believe. Not what you intend. Not what you post. Not what you wish people saw. Who are you becoming—based on what you practice, especially when you are tired, stressed, disappointed, and unobserved?

Identity is one of those words that sounds philosophical until you notice how practical it is. It shows up in your tone, your patience, your choices, your defaults, and what you reach for when you want relief. It determines what you do next, and what you do next determines what your life feels like. If you've ever looked back on a season of your life and thought, *How did I end up here?* you've already felt the power of identity, even if you didn't call it that.

A lot of people think identity is something you get: a title, a label, a tribe, a cause, a role, a public stance, a personality type, a brand. Those things can be useful, and sometimes they are even necessary. But most of the time that isn't identity—it's costume. Costumes are tempting for one simple reason: they come with belonging. If you join the right tribe and speak the right language, you get a place to stand, and in a lonely world that can feel like oxygen.

The problem is that borrowed identity rarely produces peace. It usually produces defense. Once your identity is tied to the tribe, disagreement stops feeling like information and starts feeling like threat. Questions begin to feel like betrayal. Evidence begins to feel like an attack. Deep down you know why: if the story falls apart, the belonging might fall apart with it.

This chapter is not about becoming someone fake. It is about removing what's fake so the real you can breathe again.

Identity Is a Story That Becomes a Life

Identity can be elusive if we don't think. It becomes even more elusive if we don't understand what it's like to be on the other side of us. When you lose that perspective you don't just lose self-awareness—you lose the ability to see your own patterns clearly. And when you can't see your patterns, identity becomes something you borrow instead of something you build.

Here is a working definition I've learned to trust because it is less poetic and more mechanical: identity is the story you believe about yourself, and that story determines your actions, which determines your reality. That isn't motivational; it is simply how human beings work. Your brain runs on stories whether you notice them or not. Stories tell you what's normal. Stories tell you what's possible. Stories tell you what to tolerate. Stories tell you what to fear, what to chase, and what to avoid.

That's why false identity rarely shows up as a dramatic collapse. Most of the time it shows up as a quiet drift into a story that keeps you defended, reactive, and stuck. And there is nothing sadder than a person who takes on a false identity and slowly steps out of reality while calling it "just how I am." If you want a better life, you don't start by trying to look better. You start by telling the truth about the story you are rehearsing.

The Moment I Learned a New Kind of Self-Awareness

One morning I walked into my favorite coffee shop in Chesterfield, Missouri. I showed up early, thinking I'd have a quiet start, and there at a table was my sponsor—my friend, mentor, and wise counselor—Frank. I loved meeting Frank. The conversations were stimulating, the cappuccino was sublime, and the time always felt like a good investment in my growth.

But that day I wasn't in the mood for a debate. I wanted answers. Something had me off. I wanted the kind of conversation where you lay out the problem, someone nods, tells you you're right, and you walk out feeling justified. Frank didn't do that. Frank would make me think, and sometimes I didn't want to think. Thinking takes energy. It takes humility. It takes the willingness to sit in discomfort and stare at your own assumptions.

We talked about everything: religion, politics, parenting, sales, investing, sobriety. There was nothing off-limits, and we didn't have to agree to learn from each other. Even when we did agree, Frank would sometimes take the opposite side just to test the strength of the thought. Not to win. To reveal.

After the pleasantries, Frank looked at me and said, "Jim, are you epistemologically self-aware?"

In my mind I thought, *I'm self-aware,* and my ego snapped into a defensive posture. I said yes. Then I smiled and asked, "What does that mean?" Frank patiently explained the roots of the word and then gave it to me in plain language: "How do you know what you know?"

That question sounds simple until you sit with it. It doesn't just challenge what you believe. It challenges how you arrived there—and whether you're willing to discover you might be wrong. Frank wasn't trying to make me smarter. He was trying to make me freer. Most false identities survive because we never examine the evidence we use to protect them. We treat our assumptions like facts and our feelings like truth, and then we build a life on top of them.

"How do you know what you know?" wasn't just a method for debate. It was a method for identity. It put my inner story on the table without me realizing it, and it forced a question that ego hates but growth requires: *Is this actually true, or is this just familiar?*

When Expectations Are Off, Identity Scrambles

Here's a pattern I had to face. When I'm upset about something, it's usually because I'm having trouble accepting a person, place, or thing. I want to control something outside of my control. Either there's something I cannot change, or there's an expectation I had that isn't being met. Most of the time the other party never agreed to my expectations in the first place. Often they didn't even know the expectation existed.

That's why, in recovery meetings, we always return to the Serenity Prayer. It isn't a sentimental poem. It is a leadership tool for the inner life, something that reorders your mind when your emotions are trying to run the room.

God, grant me the serenity
To accept the things I cannot change
The courage to change the things I can
And the wisdom to know the difference.

I'll say it bluntly: misaligned expectations are where drama comes from. And when reality doesn't cooperate with my expectations, my identity doesn't just get disappointed. It gets disoriented.

If I expect success and get failure, I can sulk and take on the identity of a victim. If I expect appreciation and get silence, I can take on the identity of the overlooked martyr. If I expect agreement and get resistance, I can take on the identity of the righteous one. The external event matters less than the internal reaction, because the identity shift happens fast, and it usually occurs quietly.

"If they would just…"
"No one understands how hard I'm working."
"This shouldn't be happening."
"I don't deserve this."
"I'm doing everything right."

In those moments, I'm not thinking clearly. I'm protecting something. There's usually fear under it—often irrational. Fear of losing something. Fear of being exposed. Fear of looking incompetent. Fear of losing status. Fear of being powerless. And there's usually ego under it too: pride, the need to be right, the need to be seen, the need to feel in control.

Frank had a habit that irritated my ego and helped me grow: in every situation, he brought me back to my role and what I actually had control over. Sometimes the only thing I could control was my attitude, my next right step, or my emotions about the situation. But that was enough. That's where agency begins.

False Identities Are Often "Reasonable"

We tend to think false identity means something extreme—delusional, loud, obviously broken. Sometimes it is. But more often it's subtle. It's socially acceptable. It has logic behind it. It can even sound mature.

I'm just a hard worker. I'm just stressed. I'm just someone who needs a reprieve. I'm just passionate. I'm just telling it like it is. I'm fine.

These identities don't feel fake. They feel protective. They help you cope. They help you avoid pain. They help you avoid the harder truth: you might need to change. I know this because I lived it.

For a long time, I was convinced my identity was simple: I was a non-alcoholic. And an occasional drug user. That identity came with certainty, and certainty came with insulation. Because if I "knew" I didn't have a problem, then I didn't have to grow. I didn't have to confront reality. I didn't have to face consequences. I could keep justifying, keep explaining, keep managing the story.

I had my arguments. I had my evidence. I had my comparisons. I had my excuses. I had my tribe. I had my watering holes. I had happy hours and drinking buddies—people who helped me stay inside the identity I wanted to keep.

And it wasn't that I never had doubts. There was a crack. The crack showed up when I started trying to prove I wasn't an alcoholic.

That's a sentence worth rereading.

When you find yourself working hard to prove something about yourself, you should slow down and ask why. Because the harder you have to defend an identity, the less stable it usually is.

Eventually the truth became unavoidable: I am an alcoholic. I do have a problem. One drink always leads to more. Once I start, stopping is difficult. It took a long time to see that clearly and to begin living anew. But when the identity finally shifted, something surprised me.

The relief wasn't just that I stopped drinking. The relief was that I stopped arguing.

The Exhausting Cost of Defending a False Identity

There's a kind of fatigue that comes from living in a false identity. It's not just tiredness. It's the constant mental burden of keeping reality at bay. When your identity doesn't line up with reality, you have to keep reality on trial. You have to reinterpret consequences. You have to excuse patterns. You have to blame circumstances. You have to compare yourself to worse people. You have to keep the story intact.

And that story takes energy.

In active addiction, the thoughts sounded reasonable in the moment: *I've had a really tough day. I deserve a reprieve. Everyone blows off steam. It's Friday night. I worked hard. I'm not hurting anyone. I can handle it.* That's the subtle false identity: *I'm just a guy who needs relief from stress.*

But over time I saw the vicious cycle. Much of the stress and tension I needed relief from was being caused by the very thing I was using for relief. I was drinking to escape the fire, while carrying matches in my pocket.

And that's where the identity paradox shows up: the identity you cling to for comfort becomes the identity that keeps you trapped.

The Shift From Victim to Volunteer

This is one of the most essential identity shifts I've ever made, and it applies far beyond addiction. When I'm in a victim identity, my internal script is loud. It wants a villain. It wants a courtroom. It wants a quick exit from discomfort. It wants relief, validation, control, or someone to blame.

In that state, I reach for behaviors that numb thinking: impatience, blaming, scrolling, rehearsing arguments, withdrawal, comparison. Sometimes I'm not even looking for solutions. I'm looking for escape. I tell myself, *I don't want to think about that right now. I need to get my mind off of this.* The victim identity isn't just a feeling—it's a strategy. It tries to protect me from discomfort by convincing me I'm powerless.

There's usually a moment before I realize I've slipped into that story. It's subtle. It doesn't announce itself. It just sounds reasonable. I'll be replaying a conversation in my head—something someone said that didn't sit right, a decision that affected me without my input, an outcome that feels unfair. The scene loops, and each time it does, I'm a little more justified, a little more irritated, a little more certain that the problem is out there. My body tightens. My jaw sets. My thinking narrows.

What's happening isn't analysis. It's rehearsal.

I'm rehearsing a story where I'm stuck, misunderstood, or wronged. And the strange thing is, the story feels productive. It feels like I'm working on something. But if I'm honest, nothing is actually changing. I'm just feeding the same emotional loop and calling it thinking. Sometimes I don't catch it until my mood has shifted and I'm carrying that tension into the next room, the next conversation, the next interaction with someone who had nothing to do with the original problem. That's usually the tell. When unrelated people start feeling heavier to be around, I know I've been living inside my head too long.

When I do catch it, the shift is almost embarrassingly small. I stop and ask myself a question Frank taught me to ask: *What part of this is actually mine?* Not in a self-blaming way. In a grounding way. I don't ask who's wrong. I ask where I have agency. The answer is rarely dramatic. It's often something simple and uncomfortable: I need to have a clarifying conversation. I need to adjust an expectation. I need to accept something I can't change. I need to take a next step instead of waiting for someone else to move first. Or sometimes I just need to let the feeling pass without turning it into a story.

That's when the victim script loosens its grip—not because the situation suddenly improves, but because I'm no longer pretending I'm powerless. I may not like the circumstances, but I'm no longer at their mercy. I'm not performing strength in that moment. I'm practicing responsibility.

The volunteer identity is different. It doesn't deny hardship, and it doesn't pretend pain is imaginary. It simply refuses to live as if I have no role. Volunteer identity begins when I tell a specific truth: I am the common denominator in my areas of stress. That doesn't mean everything is my fault. It means I'm involved. I'm participating. I'm making choices—sometimes wise, sometimes not—and those choices have consequences.

Volunteer identity changes the questions I ask. Instead of asking, *Why is this happening to me?* I start asking, *What can I do? What should I do? What's the next right step?* That's agency. That's adulthood. That's leadership over the self.

It's also a quieter identity. It doesn't perform. It doesn't demand applause. It doesn't need a tribe to validate it. It just moves.

Why Screens Make False Identity Harder to Shed

Screens are not neutral. They are designed to keep you longer. Videos and feeds toy with your emotions, trigger you, and pull you into deeper loops: *Watch this. Now watch this. You need to see this. You won't believe what happened. Here's what they don't want you to know.* The business model is your attention, and the method is emotional manipulation: outrage, fear, status, belonging, shock, curiosity, validation.

When you consume enough of that, you don't just lose time. You lose clarity. Your mind becomes more reactive. Your emotions become easier to steer. Your ability to sit in weakens. Your thinking gets thinner. A person can spend years "staying informed" while quietly becoming less grounded, less calm, less patient, less wise—not because they're weak, but because they are being trained.

This is why I use the phrase mental fitness.

Mental fitness is the ability to stay clear, calm, and intentional under pressure. It is emotional stamina. It is attention stamina. It is the ability to sit in discomfort long enough to tell the truth and choose your next right step. And mental fitness doesn't come from slogans. It comes from training.

There's a moment I've lived more times than I want to admit. It usually happens in the late afternoon, when the day has taken something out of me. Maybe it's a difficult call. Maybe it's a conflict I didn't ask for. Maybe it's that low-grade heaviness that comes from carrying too many responsibilities without enough margin. Nothing dramatic—just enough pressure to make my mind want relief.

I'll be standing in the kitchen, or walking through the house, and I'll reach for my phone without thinking. Not because I need anything—because I want something. I want the small hit of distraction that makes me forget the weight for a minute. I tell myself I'm just going to check one thing. A text. A headline. A score. Something harmless. Something quick.

But "quick" is almost never what happens.

One thing turns into five. Five turns into a rabbit hole. And before I know it, I'm not checking my phone—I'm being checked by it. The room gets quieter, but my mind gets noisier. My emotions start shifting in response to people I've never met and problems I can't solve. I can feel my attention thinning out like butter spread too far across bread. I'm not resting. I'm disappearing.

What makes that moment dangerous isn't that it's immoral. It's that it's automatic. It's identity in motion. It's my brain rehearsing a story: when I'm uncomfortable, I numb.

Sometimes I catch it early. I'll notice the subtle irritability, the low-grade anxiety, the strange sense that I'm "behind" even while I'm doing nothing. And if I'm honest, I'll admit what I'm really looking for. I'm not looking for information. I'm looking for relief.

That's usually the turning point. Because once I name it, I have a choice. I can keep drifting, or I can practice. So I put the phone down—sometimes it feels like setting down a small buzzing machine that wants to be held—and I do something unglamorous but real. I step outside. I take a short walk. I open a book and read one page slowly. I sit still for two minutes and let the feelings rise without trying to solve them. I write a few lines in a journal. I pick up the guitar and play a simple progression I know by heart.

None of those things are dramatic. But they are honest. They don't give me relief on credit. They strengthen something in me instead of borrowing from tomorrow. And in that small moment, I'm not just making a better decision. I'm rehearsing a different identity: when I'm uncomfortable, I notice. I choose.

So the question isn't, "Do you have self-control?" The better question is: what is training your mind right now?

Let me slow down here, because this is where readers can feel judged, and that's not my heart. Most people don't wake up and decide to lose themselves in a screen. They drift. They're tired. They're lonely. They're overwhelmed. The screen offers something immediate: stimulation, belonging, certainty, escape. It hands you relief on credit, and then it keeps collecting interest.

That's why I'm going to say something plainly, but with compassion: it is not okay to become the person who spends thirty-five hours a week mindlessly scrolling. I don't say that to shame you. I say it to tell the truth. Thirty-five hours a week isn't "a little downtime." It's nearly a full-time job. Over time it shapes the story you live inside, and it shapes the identity you rehearse.

And that raises an honest question worth sitting with: are you going to the screen because your mental fitness is low—or is constant screen consumption lowering your mental fitness over time? I'm not trying to diagnose you. I'm not offering medical advice. I'm inviting you to observe the loop.

Mental fitness works much like physical fitness. You don't lose strength overnight. You lose it gradually—by avoiding effort, avoiding resistance, and choosing the path of least challenge. And just like physical fitness, mental fitness is rebuilt through daily practices, not dramatic gestures. The goal isn't perfection. The goal is steadiness. The goal is to become the kind of person who can tell the truth and choose wisely even when life is loud.

So I want to ask you plainly: where are the stories you believe about yourself coming from? Are they coming from prayer and reflection? From reading and thinking? From real conversations with people who know you well? Or are they coming from feeds, headlines, outrage, comparison, and constant stimulation?

Because the narrator matters. The narrator shapes the story. The story shapes the identity. The identity shapes the actions. And the actions shape the life.

PRECEPT Isn't a New Costume. It's a Training Plan.

What I can tell you from my own experience is simple. A life filled with more sober-mindedness—more prayer, more reading, more exercise, more journaling, more getting off my butt, more practicing guitar, more thinking time—has given me stronger mental fitness. And with that has come more joy, more peace, and a better outlook on life. Not because life stopped being hard, but because my mind became more capable of handling it.

That's my argument. Not that this will fix everything. Not that it's easy. Not that it's quick. But that it might work for you too.

So don't treat PRECEPT as a new identity to perform. Treat it as a training plan for mental fitness. Your identity is not what you claim. It's what you practice.

A Simple Exercise: The Identity Audit (10 Minutes)

Get a pen and paper. Answer these quickly and honestly:

1. When I'm stressed, I become: _____
2. The identity I reach for is: _____
3. It protects me from feeling: _____
4. But it costs me: _____
5. The truer identity I want to practice is: _____
6. The smallest action that proves that identity today is:

   _____

Don't overthink it. The point is not to impress yourself. The point is to tell the truth, because truth is where peace begins.

Frank's Five Questions: A Mirror for Identity

Frank gave me a tool that still works when I'm tempted to drift into victim identity or tribal identity: five questions—Socratic questions—with endless variations. They are simple, and they are not easy, because they force you to think instead of react.

1. How do I know that's true?
2. What assumptions am I making?
3. What evidence would change my mind?
4. What would someone who disagrees with me say?
5. What are the logical implications of my position?

These questions expose whether my identity is grounded in truth or propped up by certainty. A tribal identity hates these questions because tribal identity needs protection, not scrutiny. Tribal identity wants slogans, not reflection. Tribal identity wants a villain, not responsibility. But a mature identity welcomes scrutiny because it would rather be free than "right." That's why these questions are not just for debate. They're for growth. They're for leadership. They're for identity.

A New Identity Statement

You don't need a long speech. You need a clear sentence you can practice—one you can return to when you feel yourself drifting.

Here's one you can borrow until you write your own:

I don't numb. I notice. I choose.

That's mental fitness in a sentence.

A Final Word

If you've read this chapter and thought, *I have identity issues,* you're not alone. When identity is unstable, purpose gets blurry, and when purpose is blurry, distraction becomes more appealing. The feed will always offer you something easier: stimulation, certainty, belonging, and escape. It will offer you a costume that fits quickly, a tribe that feels like home, and a story that doesn't require much change.

But peace isn't found in the feed. Peace is found when your story matches reality—when your practices align with your purpose—and that requires your attention. It requires you to tell the truth, not once, but repeatedly, until truth becomes your default.

So here is the question again, where we began, and where you'll return a thousand times in small moments that don't look important until they add up into a life:

Who are you becoming?

Not based on what you hope. Not based on what you say. Based on what you practice.

You're not trying to become someone else. You're taking your life back.

———

IDENTITY IS TRAINING

Identity isn't what you say about yourself. It's what your brain rehearses. What you practice becomes your default. PRECEPT is a training plan for mental fitness.

POINTS TO REMEMBER

Identity is the story you believe about yourself, and that story shapes your actions and your reality. Many false identities are subtle and "reasonable," but they quietly pull you out of reality and into defensiveness. Screens intensify this by training reactivity, comparison, and emotional dependence, which lowers mental fitness over time. The path forward isn't shame—it's training. PRECEPT isn't a new costume to perform; it's a set of practices that rebuild mental fitness and help you become steadier, freer, and more grounded.

A Final Invitation

I f this book helped you—if it gave you language for something you've been feeling, or helped you notice how distracted your life had quietly become—I would appreciate an honest review.

Not because I need praise, but because reviews help this message reach people who are right where you may have been when you started reading. People who feel tired, scattered, reactive, and quietly frustrated with themselves—but don't yet know why. Your words may be the thing that helps someone else wake up.

You'll find a QR code near the back of this book. If you're willing, take a moment to scan it and leave a short, honest review. A few sentences is enough. Thank you for taking the time.

And before you close this book for good, I want to encourage one more thing—not as an obligation, but as a gift to yourself.

Keep the Practice Going

Reading can wake us up.

But practice is what changes us.

If PRECEPT resonated with you, the next step isn't to read another book. It's to create space—daily, intentional space—where your mind can slow down, notice, and choose. That's why I created the **UNHIJACKED Journal Series**.

These are not motivational journals. They are not about affirmations, hype, or forcing positivity. They are **simple daily practices** designed to help you take your attention back, one small moment at a time.

Each journal focuses on a different kind of mental fitness:

- **Unhijacked: Gratitude**
  - A daily practice for calm, clarity, and perspective—training your mind to notice what's real and good instead of what's loud and missing.
- **Unhijacked: Prayer & Presence**
  - A structured space for stillness, focus, and quiet connection—especially for those who want their faith to feel less rushed and more grounded.
- **Unhijacked: Capture the Day**
  - A reflection practice for awareness and emotional calm—helping you observe your thoughts and experiences without being swallowed by them.
- **Unhijacked: Goals That Stick**
  - A discipline-first approach to habits and follow-through—designed for people who are tired of setting goals and quietly abandoning them. And for those who want a single, unified place to begin, there is a flagship journal:
- **Unhijacked: The Daily Practice**
  - An intentional system for taking back control of your mind and life— bringing gratitude, reflection, prayer, and discipline into one calm, repeatable rhythm.

You don't need all of them. You don't need to do them perfectly. You don't even need to do them every day at first.

You just need a place to return to.

Because that's what this whole book has been about—not becoming someone new, but returning to yourself. Returning to clarity. Returning to agency. Returning to the part of you that can notice, choose, and live on purpose.

If you decide to pick up a journal, let it be a place where you practice telling the truth. A place where your mind can slow down enough to hear itself again. A place where your attention stops being hijacked and starts becoming yours.

Thank you for reading.

Thank you for staying with the work.

And thank you for choosing to take your life back—one practice at a time.

If this book resonated with you—if it helped you notice where your attention has been drifting or gave language to something you've been feeling—I would be grateful for an honest review. You'll find a QR code on the next page; a few sentences can help this message reach someone who needs it. And if you're ready to keep the work going, consider starting a daily practice with one of the UNHIJACKED journals. They aren't motivational or performative—they're simple, intentional tools for slowing your mind, noticing what's real, and rebuilding mental fitness through gratitude, reflection, prayer, and disciplined follow-through. You don't need to do it perfectly; you just need a place to return to. That's how attention is reclaimed—and how a life is quietly taken back.

Thank You for Reading

If you're reading this, it means you made it all the way through the book—and I don't take that lightly. I'm genuinely grateful you invested your time, attention, and thought here.

If this book challenged you, encouraged you, or helped you see leadership differently, would you be willing to help others by sharing your perspective?

Your review doesn't have to be long or polished.

It simply helps future readers understand what this book meant to *you*.

Scan here to leave a review on Amazon

BRING THIS CONVERSATION TO YOUR ORGANIZATION

The ideas in this book come alive when leaders experience them together.

I work with organizations that want less drama, clearer communication, and leadership that actually works in the real world. If you're looking for a speaker who connects deeply, challenges thinking, and leaves people changed—not just motivated—I'd love to continue the conversation.

Scan here to learn more about booking Jim Koetting to speak

Acknowledgements

This book would not exist without the patience, love, and steady support of my wife, **Barb**, my partner of 32 years. She stood by me while I disappeared into the zone—keyboard clicking, headphones on, mentally somewhere else—giving me the space and grace to do the work. Her quiet strength and unwavering belief in me made this possible.

I am deeply grateful to my daughters, **Morgan and Madi**. They are both exceptional writers and remarkable women. Their encouragement, insight, and love mean more to me than they will ever fully know. Watching the women they have become is one of the great privileges of my life.

I want to thank my mentor, spiritual advisor, friend, and adopted big brother **Jim Zilinsky**, along with the many sponsors, coaches, and mentors who have invested in me over the years. Each of you shaped my thinking, challenged my assumptions, and helped me grow when growth was uncomfortable but necessary.

I am also thankful to the organizations that have invited me to speak and share these ideas. Your trust gave these concepts a place to be tested, refined, and lived out in the real world.

To the **mentees** who chose me as a mentor, and to my **coaching and consulting clients** who trusted me to walk alongside them as they grew—thank you. I have learned as much from you as you have from me. Through coaching, counseling, problem-solving, and consulting together, we grew side by side.

This book is as much a reflection of those relationships as it is of my own journey.

About the Author

JIM KOETTING is a speaker, mentor, and leadership advisor who thrives on connecting with large audiences and helping people increase their influence—at work, at home, and in life.

Jim's perspective is shaped by an uncommon mix of experiences. He has built businesses, led and scaled software teams in the United States and internationally, and written a book on managing risk in fixed-income investing. His work has put him in rooms with presidents and billionaire business leaders—including an invitation to the Oval Office—and on stages where ideas are tested not in theory, but in real life.

Equally formative are the parts of his story that never show up on a résumé. Jim has been sober for 36 years, an experience that deeply informs his understanding of discipline, distraction, human behavior, and sustainable performance. He is an avid scuba diver, a lifelong student of focus and presence, and a musician of more than 50 years who has played in bands and learned firsthand how leadership, timing, listening, and trust determine whether a group falls apart—or becomes something greater than the sum of its parts.

Jim is known for his ability to blend storytelling, hard-earned wisdom, and practical insight into talks that are engaging, honest, and immediately useful. He doesn't speak at audiences—he brings them into the conversation, challenging assumptions while creating space for reflection and growth.

At the core of Jim's work is a simple belief: influence isn't about titles, authority, or charisma—it's about awareness, intention, and the discipline to live what you teach. Whether speaking to executives, entrepreneurs, or emerging leaders, Jim's goal is always the same—to leave people thinking differently about how they show up, and better equipped to lead.

Jim lives in Kansas City with his wife, Barb, and remains endlessly grateful for his two daughters, Morgan and Madison."

Index